Understanding
Cricket

Understanding Cricket

by
Bernard Whimpress

Illustrations by
Bob Dikkenberg

ISBN: 1 86476 378 7

Copyright © Axiom Publishing, 2006.
First published 1985, revised edition 2006.
Unit 2, 1 Union Street, Stepney, South Australia 5069

Text Copyright © Bernard Whimpress 2006.

AXIOM
AUSTRALIA

www.axiompublishing.com.au

Printed in Malaysia

Bernard Whimpress is Curator of the Adelaide Oval Museum. He has written 12 books on sport, including *Passport to Nowhere: Aborigines in Australian Cricket 1850-1939* and *Chuckers: A History of Throwing in Australian Cricket*. Last year he compiled *The Superior Cricket Watcher's Ashes Quiz Book* and most recently updated *Great Ashes Battles*. His writing is much better than his play. His batting was so stodgy that at school he once occupied the crease every lunch hour for a week while making 22 runs. As a bowler he thought he was the logical successor to Richie Benaud but fell a long way short.

Illustrator, **Bob Dikkenberg** is the cartoonist for the Australian Defence Force newspapers. He is a military mapmaker who has been to some of the remotest parts of the planet. As a cricketer, his batting leaves something to be desired. Any runs he gets he likens it to the Indians in a John Wayne movie in that while they look good you know that they won't last long. His bowling is feed for the sightboard and a danger to the crowd not unlike the short sighted javelin thrower in the Flinders Island Games in 1962. He is married with two sons who have been fortunate not to inherit his cricketing gene.

The Riddle of Cricket

You have two sides: one out in the field and one in.

Each man that's in the side that's in goes out, and when he's out he comes in and the next man goes in until he's out.

When they are all out, the side that's out comes in and the side that's been in goes out and tries to get those coming in out.

Sometimes you get men still in and not out.

When both sides have been in and out, including the not outs, that's the end of the game.

Contents

Introduction

This book has been written for two types of cricket watchers in Australia: those who are new to the game and those uncertain of its finer points.

Most of today's cricket watchers have had their interest sparked by watching the game on television, and this book is intended to further their knowledge gained from that medium.

Today's television spectator is spoilt. He or she has a position behind the bowler's arm (from each end), the advantage of close-up zoom cameras to examine movements in great detail, a range of other views taken from side on and around the ground to bring *atmosphere* into the lounge room. And as if that is not enough, he has action replays of major incidents heightening his awareness of the climaxes of play, with expert comments by a team of former Test captains and players.

The television cricket watcher may appear to have it all, but this does not mean that he *knows or understands* it all. Cricket is in many respects a legacy of an earlier age, with its drama unfolding slowly. It can, of course, be exciting when runs, wickets, and time are factors in a chase for victory, but it often hides behind its own mystique, projecting subtleties for slow play.

One of the difficulties for the new cricket watcher is that the pervasive (some might say invasive) influence of television has made him an *instant expert*, when in truth there is no substitute for *slow learning* and the development of memory in order to compare and contrast conditions and judge players' performances.

This book will serve two purposes. It will define and provoke thought, explain (in brief) the origins and history of the game, the most important details of play, and the laws governing it, as well as various tactical considerations.

People watch cricket for many reasons, and there is much enjoyment to be gained from watching. It takes time for observers who are new to the game to appreciate the skills and styles of batsmen and bowlers, to realise that the playing conditions in the weather and nature of the wicket greatly affect performance, and that a player's effectiveness cannot be measured simply by runs and wickets on the scorecard.

1

A Brief History

Like many bat and ball games, cricket evolved slowly from obscure origins. It has been suggested that it was first played in forests where tree *stumps* became a natural target. The first bats were often simply branches of a tree and were described by an Anglo-Saxon word *cricce* meaning 'not quite straight'. The game possibly derived its name from this source, although there are other clues in the Old English word *batt* meaning staff and bail from the Old French word *beil*, a horizontal piece of wood placed on two uprights.

From the very beginning cricket has combined the elements of attack and defence: the batsman defending the target area against the bowler.

The *wicket* was a type of hoop similar to the entrance of a sheep pen and dates from about 1700. The two uprights and single bail were altered

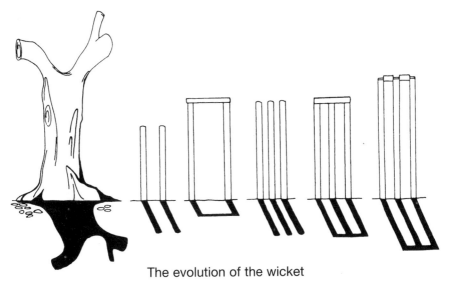

The evolution of the wicket

with the addition of a middle stump in 1776 after an unfortunate bowler, 'Lumpy' Stevens of Kent, bowled several balls 'through the gate'. Ten years later a second bail was added for the wicket to take on its present-day appearance.

The late eighteenth century saw cricket begin to standardise some of its measures. A ball was to weigh between 5½ and 5¾ ounces (156-163 grams) and a bat to be no wider than 4¼ inches (10.8 cm), the same as today. Following the formation of the Marylebone Cricket Club (MCC) laws were formalised, such as lbw and hit-wicket as means of dismissal.

At this stage of its development, cricket had expanded from a game played by agricultural labourers to one which attracted the interest and patronage of the aristocratic and new business classes. In the great age of British imperialism in the nineteenth century, it was carried to the far-flung extremities of the Empire.

The first organised game was played by the soldiers of the ship, HMS *Calcutta*, at a site that is now Hyde Park, Sydney, in 1803, eleven years before the first game was played by the MCC at Lord's. Cricket spread through the Australian colonies and the introduction of round-arm bowling in England in 1835 was quickly adopted as a replacement for the earlier under-arm bowling.

Two other factors also encouraged the game's growth. The Duke of Wellington, as commander-in-chief of Britain's armed forces, ordered cricket pitches to be laid alongside every military barracks and there was a strong correlation between cricket and the hotel trade.

The first English cricket tour to Australia, led by H.H. Stephenson, was organised and promoted by the Melbourne catering firm of Spiers & Pond in 1861 and met with little opposition. Nearly all the matches were played against twenty-two opponents, and the Australians were good companions. Roger Iddison of Yorkshire made one of the game's most memorable quotes when he returned home: 'I don't think much of their play but they're a wonderful lot of drinking men.'

George Parr, three years later, and W.G. Grace in 1873-74, led teams to Australia before James Lillywhite's side in 1876-77 played the first Test matches in Melbourne.

Although the Ashes were not born until five years later, Anglo-Australian Tests became the cornerstone of international cricket and a national Australian team preceded the Federal Commonwealth.

After the 1891-92 tour the game received a tremendous impetus in Australia with the donation of the Sheffield Shield for contests between the colonies of New South Wales, Victoria and South Australia. Similar impetus in England had followed the introduction of the County Championship and overarm bowling in 1864.

In the Cape Colony, South Africa, cricket was again founded by the British Army and spread through the rest of the provinces of Natal, Orange Free State and Transvaal with the Currie Cup domestic competition beginning in 1889-90, changing its name to the Castle Cup in 1990-91 and to the SuperSport Series in 1996-97.

The slowness of sea travel halted development in West Indian cricket, and the regular inter-island competition, the Shell Shield which gave way to the Red Stripe, President's, Busta and Caribbean Cups only dates from 1965-66 even though West Indian Test teams have existed since 1928.

New Zealand cricket did not begin until the second half of the nineteenth century when George Parr's team played four matches there after completing their Australian tour, and Lillywhite's team also visited the country in 1877. Dave Gregory's 1878 team to England also crossed the Tasman before starting its voyage. The Plunket Shield for matches between the provinces was first contested in 1921-22 before changing its name to the Shell Trophy and then the State Championship.

Cricket languished in India for a long time owing to warfare, and patronage passed from the British Raj to the Indian aristocracy and on to modern industry and commerce. For the early part of the twentieth century the main matches were contests organised on communal and religious lines and eventually known as the Pentangular when it consisted of teams representing the Europeans, Parsees, Hindus, Mohammedans and The Rest. The Ranji Trophy, named after Prince Kumar Shri Ranjitsinhji who starred for England around the turn of the twentieth century, was introduced in 1934-35.

Pakistani cricket existed only in name following the creation of that country in 1947 following Indian partition, but commenced Test cricket within five years. The major domestic competition is the Quaid-E-Azam Trophy which was first contested in 1953-54.

Sri Lanka has a long cricket history from the time when it was known as Ceylon but the first-class domestic competition has been strengthened in recent years with the Lakspray Trophy beginning in 1988-89 succeeded by the P. Saravanamuttu and Premier's Trophies.

Zimbabwe (as Rhodesia) played for many years in South Africa's Currie Cup competition but its main domestic competition, the Logan Cup, has been operating only since 1993-94.

Bangladesh (as East Pakistan) played host to a Test match at Dhaka in 1959. However, a modern National Cricket League was only established in 2000-01.

Australia's cricket heroes were immediate: Charles Bannerman, whose innings of 165 dominated the first-ever Test match; William Murdoch, a great batsman and first to top 200 in a Test; Frederick 'Demon' Spofforth, the man whose 14 wickets for 90 runs humiliated England in the 'Ashes' match of 1882; George Giffen, the world's best all-rounder of the nineteenth century; and Jack Blackham, an excellent wicket-keeper, all traded punches with the man simply described as The Champion – Dr W.G. Grace.

It was said that until relatively recently the history of international cricket could be linked from Grace to Hobbs to Hutton to Sobers to Imran Khan, but such neatness is easily shattered. The years 1928-48 were unmistakeably dubbed the Bradman Era, despite any overlap by Hobbs, Hammond, Headley, or Hutton, and Victor Trumper was the undisputed king of Australian cricket in the years before the First World War.

The reader who so wishes can take her own trip down memory lane but it is interesting to note the amount of international cricket played at the present time compared with the past. For example, up to the Second

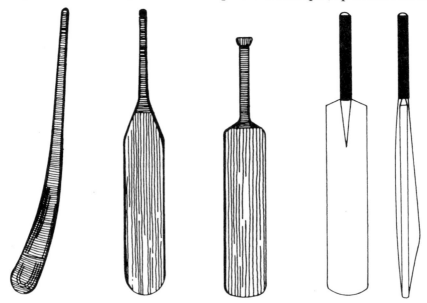

Changing styles of bats from the early hockey stick shape to today

World War only two other Test-playing sides visited Australia apart from England; South Africa in 1910-11 and 1931-32, and the West Indies in 1931-32.

Since the Second World War, India came here in 1947-48, but after the West Indian (1951-52) and South African (1952-53) touring teams, invitations wee again extended only to Englishmen until 1960-61.

The West Indian team that summer was led by Frank Worrell and it proved to be one of the most exciting and attractive series of all time. It was also one which changed public favour to the West Indies because of their dash and panache in strong contrast to the dour tactics employed by Englishmen.

Even so, two English teams came to Australia in 1962-63 and 1965-66, the South Africans in 1963-64, Pakistan for a solitary Test in 1964-65, India for a four Test series in 1967-68, and the West Indies not again until 1968-69.

The 1969-70 season was the last purely domestic one in Australia and every Test-playing country has toured since. In the last two years Bangladesh, Zimbabwe, India, Sri Lanka, New Zealand and Pakistan have all played Test matches in Australia.

The biggest influence on the modern game has, however, been the introduction of one-day limited over cricket. The first limited over international match was played between Australia and England in 1970-71 and by the end of the 2005-06 Australian summer there had been 2366 more, of which Australia had contested 615 games. The first Prudential World Cup limited over competition was staged in England in 1975 and proved such a great success that seven more have followed.

The real expansion of one-day cricket came during the split between Kerry Packer's World Series Cricket and the traditional game, and this has been maintained first under the guidance of Packer's company PBL Marketing from 1979-80 and subsequently by the Australian Cricket Board and Cricket Australia since 1994.

A fuller discussion of limited over cricket is given in Chapter 10, and while it has been seen as the saviour of the game, the view has often been expressed that it has reached saturation point.

The continued survival of cricket was precarious for a long time but despite commercial windfalls from television fears remain that administrators might kill the goose that lays the golden egg. Further overkill may follow the programming of Twenty/20 cricket.

2

The Game's Essentials

The object of playing cricket is for one side to score more runs than its opponents. A side can only score while it is batting, and the action of batting is called an *innings*.

Cricket matches begin when the captains of two teams toss a coin to decide which side will bat first. The winner has the choice of doing so, but he may ask the other side to bat first.

When a decision is made, the side which is not batting sends its players on to the field and they are known as the *fielding side*. There are eleven such players, one of whom wears gloves and pads and is known as the *wicket-keeper*.

The fielding captain then asks one of the ten remaining players to open the bowling, and he (or she) and the *bowler* usually place the fielders in position. The wicket-keeper goes directly behind the stumps at the opposite end of the pitch to the bowler.

Two umpires also take up their positions, one at the bowler's end and the other square to the wicket at the batsman's end.

While this is happening, two members of the batting side approach the wicket to open their team's innings, with the batting captain deciding the order in which the team will bat. One of the batsmen (the *striker*) goes to the end to receive the first ball from the bowler while the *non-striker* stands behind the popping crease (see page 22) at the bowler's end.

To start the match, the umpire at the bowler's end checks whether the batsmen, bowler, fielders, and scorers are ready, notifies the striker regarding the bowler's action, hands the bowler a new ball, and calls 'play'.

Cricket is a game full of paradox. While it is variously described as subtle, intricate, and profound, it is also essentially simple: a target game between a bowler who aims his deliveries at a wicket defended by a batsman. The batsman, however, also has to strike the ball far enough to allow himself and his fellow batsman to make runs. The game becomes more intriguing because of its checks and balances, plus the range of variables which allow batsmen and bowlers to be offensive or defensive, to mount an attack and counter it.

The bowler has at his command nine fieldsmen and a wicket-keeper to assist him, and most variations are made in the arrangements of the field. Each bowler bowls six balls from one end and this called an *over*. When an over is completed the fieldsmen change ends and the next over is delivered from the other end.

Those new to cricket often find its terminology confusing but none more than the positions in the field. The field has no precise measurements although a boundary line is usually at least 70 metres from the pitch for senior matches. It is divided into *off* and *on sides* with *leg side* being an alternative name for the latter.

Off Side

The side to which the batsman faces.

Slips

Behind-the-wicket positions used especially by fast bowlers to take catches which fly from the edge of the bat. First slip is the finest and deepest of the slips and closest to the wicket-keeper. The others fan around in an arc, each one wider and squarer of the wicket. Four slips are usually the maximum number employed. Alertness and agility are the keys to slips fielding. Bob Simpson was an outstanding first slip and Ian Chappell and Mark Taylor both highly efficient, Taylor especially so to the leg-spin of Shane Warne. All three men captained Australia and found it an excellent position from which to observe the game. Warne occupies the position to the current Australian pace attack. At second slip Greg Chappell and the phenomenal Mark Waugh have given brilliant service.

Gully

A position close to the bat and slightly behind point. The gully fieldsman is often required to take the hardest catches in the game as balls which fly to him are often slashed off the middle of the bat. Australia has had a fine succession of gully fieldsmen.

Point

A position square of the stumps or popping crease and medium distance from the bat. Steve Waugh patrolled this area for much of his career.

Third man

Usually a run-saving position behind slips and gully, although it is sometimes a shorter position. *Fly slip* is used to catch batsmen whose off-side driving is insecure against a moving ball.

Covers

The three positions *cover point, cover* and *extra cover* are in the area between point and mid-off. Cover fieldsmen are normally the most brilliant outfielders: fast movers with safe hands and fast accurate throws. The South African Jonty Rhodes has been the best cover fielder in the modern era.

Mid-off

The position nearest the bowler on the off side, and the fieldsman who frequently offers words of encouragement to his team-mate. The position is usually slightly deeper than the wicket at the bowler's end.

Silly point (or Silly mid-off)

Attacking positions which are dangerously close to the bat. As with the short legs fielders often wear helmets and shin guards for protection.

Deep or long positions

Those which are defensive in intent, and aim to reduce run scoring or effect a dismissal through a mistimed stroke which falls safely into the hands of a fielder.

On or Leg Side

The side of the field nearest the batsman's legs.

Mid-on

The position nearest to the batsman on the on side of the wicket and slightly deeper than the bowler's wicket.

Mid wicket

Midway between mid-on and square leg.

Square leg

To the rear of the batsman and level with the popping crease. Alongside the square leg umpire in most cases.

Short leg

Close-catching position on the leg side which is also dangerous because it is in close proximity to the most powerful strokes in the game. Usually employed against batsmen shielding themselves from a hostile pace attack, or by slow bowlers aiming for a bat-pad catch. Short leg positions may be *square, forward* or *backward* of the popping crease.

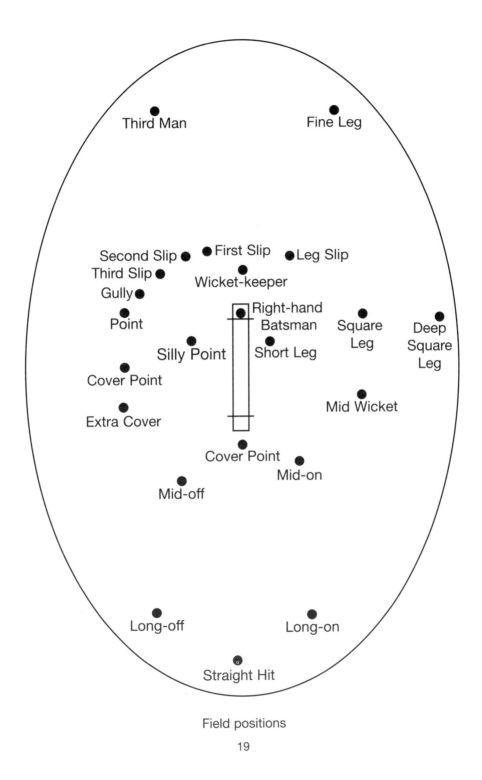

Field positions

Leg slip

A fine close to the wicket position on the leg side, but rarely used in modern-day field settings.

Fine leg

A run-saving position behind leg slip usually frequented by pace bowlers when out of the attack. During the 1980s and 1990s Craig McDermott returned the ball powerfully and accurately from the deep and Glenn McGrath made a freak diving catch against England near the end of the Adelaide Oval Test of 2002-03.

Silly mid-on (or *Silly leg*)

Often difficult to distinguish from *forward short leg* and endangered by the batsman necessitating the use of a helmet by the fielder.

Long leg

An expression rarely used, but usually taken to mean a position on the boundary between deep fine leg and deep square leg.

Leg trap

A term used to describe the employment of two or more short legs in order to bring about the downfall of a batsman.

The Pitch

The pitch is always the focus of attention, and for the purpose of this book it consists of mown turf. In lower forms of cricket, pitches may be made of concrete, malthoid, or clay, sometimes with a coir or canvas matting stretched over them. The pitch area extends between the two wickets (a term mentioned in the previous chapter), a distance of 20.12 metres (22 yards) and is 3.04 metres (10 feet) wide.

Each *wicket* is erected in the centre of a line known as the bowling crease and is 71.1 cm (28 inches) high and 22.86 cm (9 inches) wide. To complicate matters, a wicket is often referred to as 'the stumps' and is also frequently used to describe a pitch.

The creases are lines drawn on the pitch to designate where batsmen may take their stance (also known as taking guard), and bowlers deliver the ball. The *bowling crease* is in line with the stumps and measures 2.64 metres (8 feet 8 inches).

The *popping crease* runs parallel to the bowling crease and is 1.22 metres (4 feet) in front of it. It must extend to a minimum of 1.83 metres (6 feet) either side of the centre of the wicket. A bowler who oversteps the crease will be no-balled (see page 22), and it is the dividing line between safe and unsafe ground for the batsman when the ball is in play.

The *return creases* run perpendicular to the other creases from the popping crease and extend at least 1.22 metres (4 feet) behind the wicket. A bowler must have his back foot within these creases or risk being no-balled.

Getting Out

There are ten ways of getting a batsman out.

Bowled

When the ball hits the wicket and causes a bail to be dislodged, even though it may have already touched the bat, body, or clothing of the batsman. This is often the most spectacular form of dismissal when a fast bowler knocks a stump out of the ground and sends it cartwheeling towards the wicket-keeper or when a big-spinning leg break delivered by bowlers such as Shane Warne or Stuart MacGill are pitched wide of the leg stump and bowl the batsman behind his legs.

Timed out

If a batsman takes more than two minutes to reach the crease after the fall of the previous wicket. This law was introduced to prevent time wasting but has never been invoked in the first-class game.

Caught

When the ball strikes the batsman's bat, hand or glove holding the bat below the wrist, and is held by a fieldsman before it touches the ground, and within the area designated as the playing field. A catch may also be made by one fielder deflecting the ball to another who may complete it. A very famous example of a deflected catch was made by English all-rounder Geoff Miller at Melbourne in the 1982-83 series, when he ran from first slip behind Chris Tavare at second slip after Tavare knocked the ball over his head. The catch enabled England to win the match by three runs after a last wicket partnership by Allan Border and Jeff Thomson had added 70 runs. Miller's catch also gave Ian Botham his 100th Test wicket against Australia. An unfortunate dismissal was experienced by English opening batsman Marcus Trescothick when he swept a ball into Matthew Hayden's shin guard at short leg during the Headingley Test of 2001 and the ball flipped up in the air for a simple catch. Without the guard Hayden may well have suffered a broken bone in his foot and Trescothick gone on to a bigger score.

Handled the ball

Either batsman may be out by this means if he willfully touches the ball while it is in play with the hand not holding the ball, unless he first has permission of the opposing side to do. The most notorious example

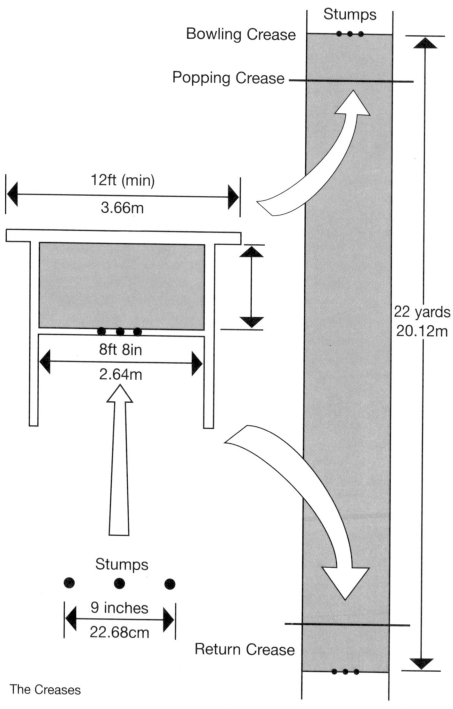

Bowling Crease

Popping Crease

Stumps

12ft (min)
3.66m

8ft 8in
2.64m

22 yards
20.12m

Stumps

9 inches
22.68cm

Return Crease

The Creases

22

of a batsman being dismissed by this means occurred in the Second Test against Pakistan in Perth in 1979 when pace bowler Sarfraz Nawaz appealed successfully against Andrew Hilditch after Hilditch had picked up the ball and returned it to him gently. A rare but fairer dismissal was that of Graham Gooch who was out for 133 at Old Trafford in 1993 when he instinctively attempted to prevent playing a ball from Merv Hughes on to his stumps by knocking it away with his hand. The dismissal is recorded 'handled the ball' on the scorecard and no credit is given to the bowler.

Hit the ball twice

If the second stroke is any other than in protection of his wicket. Courteously tapping the ball to a bowler of fielder will bring dismissal on appeal.

Hit wicket

If in the action of making a stroke or setting off for his first run the batsman breaks the wicket with his bat, body or equipment. A famous hit wicket decision was that of West Indian middle-order batsman Joe Solomon in the Second Test at Melbourne in 1960-61. In playing a stroke against Australian captain Richie Benaud, Solomon's cap fell on top of his stumps and dislodged the bails, bringing about his dismissal and raising the ire of the crowd against Benaud.

Leg before wicket (Lbw)

The most contentious means of dismissal in the game. Its aim is to reduce one of cricket's ugliest sights – deliberate pad play – by encouraging batsmen to defend their wickets with their bats. The present law still favours batsmen, in that the element of doubt surrounding decisions means they are given not out. On the other hand the law has been improved with the provision for batsmen being dismissed by balls pitched outside the off stump and coming into the bat, even though it is not so generous to bowlers whose deliveries leave the bat.

A batsman may be dismissed in the following ways. By using any part of his body or equipment, except his bat, to intercept balls which would have hit his wicket, provided that:

(1) The ball was pitched in a straight line between the wickets.

(2) The ball pitched to the off side of the striker's stumps.

(3) The point where the batsman intercepted the ball is between the wickets.

(4) The ball pitched outside the off stump, but the striker made no attempt to play the ball.

The Lbw Rule

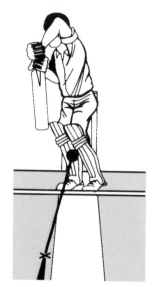

(1) The batsman is OUT if the ball is pitched outside the off stump but no stroke id offered.

(2) OUT if pitched outside the off stump but would have hit the wicket.

(3) OUT if pitched on the line of the stump and would have hit the wicket.

(4) NOT OUT if pitched outside the line of leg stump.

The batsman is not out to balls which are intercepted in line with the wicket, but when the ball is pitched outside the leg stump.

A controversial lbw decision was given against star Indian top-order batsman Sachin Tendulkar in the Adelaide Test of 1999 when he was given out to a short ball from Glenn McGrath which he ducked very low and was struck on the helmet.

Obstructing the field

Either batsman may be out if he willfully obstructs the other side by word or action. The striker shall be out if either batsman prevents a catch being made, or if the striker is legally protecting his own wicket. In 1951 English opening batsman Len Hutton was dismissed in such circumstances in the Fifth Test against South Africa at Kennington Oval.

Receiving a ball from off-spinner Athol Rowan which lifted and hit him on the glove Hutton reacted instinctively and waved his bat again at the ball in an effort to prevent it hitting his wicket. In doing so, however, he obstructed the wicket-keeper from making a catch and was given out on appeal.

The author also recalls an incident from his own experience involving a Scottish schoolteacher (and new cricket devotee at the time) who was a member of a country high school team which played weekend matches in the local town association.

Scotty was as keen as mustard and while batting he cocked up an easy catch to silly mid-off. As the fieldsman prepared to take it Scotty advanced in his direction waving his bat aggressively and crying "You'll miss it! You'll miss it!" The startled fieldsman then dropped the chance but no other appeal was made. I was the non-striker and told the fielding captain they could appeal for 'obstructing the field' but he was ignorant of the law and Scotty survived, although not much longer.

Run out

If the wicket is broken when a batsman is out of his ground and the ball is in play. If the batsmen have crossed, the one running to the wicket which is broken is out, but if the batsmen are running and have not crossed it is the batsman running from the broken wicket or is closest to it who is out. In some cases, two batsmen find themselves at the same end of the pitch with the wicket broken at the other end. In such circumstances the batsman who has remained within or returned to his crease is safe, but the one who joins him there is out.

Stumped

When a batsman is out of his ground after having received a ball and the wicket-keeper breaks the stumps with the ball in his hand, or if the ball rebounds on to the stumps from the wicket-keeper's body. The batsman must not be attempting a run in the first instance, otherwise such a dismissal will be recorded as a run out. The wicket-keeper may take the ball in front of the wicket in an effort to stump the batsman, only if it has touched his bat or body. It is important to remember *that on the line* is out and that some part of the batsman's body or bat must be *behind* the crease to be safe.

Sightscreens

Sightscreens are used to improve the batsman's sight of the ball and are located beyond the boundary in a direct line behind the wicket. The screens are usually on wheels and an attendant pushes the screen from side to side depending on the line of attack of the bowler and a request made by the batsman.

In recent years sightscreens have been used to display advertising electronically when play is at the other end and occasional breakdowns have caused interruptions to play.

Punch c1920
AMERICAN VISITOR (having had bowling-screen explained) "But my *boy*, what a chance for an *advertisement* stunt!"

3

Types of Wicket

In order to understand cricket better it is necessary to know that the behaviour of a wicket (or pitch) is the most interesting variable on which fluctuations in the game depend.

A *good wicket* is one which is well prepared, which allows a batsman to play his strokes with confidence, and yet provides assistance for the bowler who is willing to work. In real terms climatic factors govern the amount of work a curator can put into a wicket but he must aim at preparing a surface which will last four days for Pura Cup matches and five days for Test matches.

At the outset this means producing a wicket which favours batsmen and rewards the team which wins the toss. Captains like to know what sort of preparation a wicket has had because their tactics will be based on the way it plays.

A spectator's enjoyment of cricket is often enhanced if he knows the characteristics of a wicket. Wickets often maintain their character for years but may be changed by the deliberate policies of their ground committee and curator.

The best type of wicket is often described as a *good cricket wicket*: one which allows batsmen to play their strokes because the ball comes onto the bat quickly, but also gives bowlers a chance by enabling them to extract lift and movement off the pitch.

On the other hand, a *good batting wicket* is frequently easy paced, giving the bowlers little chance of making breakthroughs. On such wickets runs are usually scored at a good rate.

Green or *green-top wickets* have fast and seam bowlers licking their lips with anticipation as the ball will lift awkwardly from a good length and move off the seam. Many wickets are lively on the first morning of a first-class match, and captains who possess a hostile opening attack frequently seek an advantage on winning the toss by putting their opponents in to bat in the hope of breaking the back of their batting in the first innings. Such decisions are usually agonising because if the bowlers fail to achieve a sufficient breakthrough the batsmen then have to bat last on a pitch which may have worn.

Another point about green wickets is that humid weather conditions, which contribute to their state, also assist swing bowling so that batsmen may have to counter balls which move one way through the air and then break back off the pitch.

The liveliest wicket in Australia is in Perth where pace bowlers such as Dennis Lillee, Jeff Thomson, Andy Roberts, Michael Holding, Curtley Ambrose, Glenn McGrath and Jason Gillespie have reaped a rich harvest in the last thirty years. In the later afternoon the advent of a sea breeze, the Fremantle Doctor, also allowed Western Australian swing bowlers like Bob Massie, Ian Brayshaw, Mick Malone and Terry Alderman to wreak havoc on visiting sides over many years.

Dry, crumbling wickets occur when wickets have not had enough moisture in their preparation and crack under a dry climate. Such conditions favour spin bowlers because batsmen have no idea how much the ball will spin or bounce. A rare dusty wicket at Adelaide Oval in 2001 enabled off-spinner Colin Miller to turn in a match-winning performance when he gathered ten wickets in Australia's five wicket victory over the West Indies.

A *sticky wicket* is a term which has practically fallen out of the cricketing vocabulary since wickets have been covered over the last fifty years. Previously, if rain fell on a wicket and it was then dried by hot sun a crust developed on the surface which spin and sometimes medium-pace bowlers were able to exploit to the full.

Brisbane's tropical climate resulted in a number of such wickets, and caused Australia to be dismissed for 66 and 58 in its second innings in the 1928-29 and 1936-37 Test series against England, and India to be dismissed for 58 and 98 with Ernie Toshack taking 11 wickets for 31 runs in the First Test of their 1947-48 tour. The 1950-51 series against England opened at Brisbane with Australia being dismissed on a good wicket for 228 but a violent thunderstorm ruined it and the following day was washed out without a ball being bowled. The third day was then marked by two declarations and the total eclipse of the bat by the ball. England declared at 7 for 68, Australia then lost 7 wickets for 32 runs before closing its innings, and England lost another 6 wickets for 30 runs before the end of play.

The only vague similarity to a sticky wicket is a *wet wicket* when moisture seeps under the covers and sweats before their removal. Sometimes only part of such a wicket is affected as happened at Adelaide in the 1974-75 Ashes series, enabling English left-arm spinner Derek Underwood to make early breakthroughs in the Australian batting order. A sharp shower during play may put some life back into a wicket and cause the ball to skid through but such an advantage is often negated by bowlers having to operate with a greasy ball.

Featherbed wickets create dull cricket with batsmen complaining of timing errors owing to the ball not coming onto the bat quickly enough, and bowlers unable to extract life or quick turn from the pitch.

Good wickets must always be the main concern of administrators and grounds staff because only then can spectators see play of the highest quality.

4

A Batsman's Pleasure

Cricket has often been described as a batsman's game and cricket watchers have always been thrilled by the player who scores freely and with a wide variety of strokes. This is not to say that spectators do not appreciate the bowler's skills, and other considerations which may require the batsman to defend his wicket or occupy the crease for long periods, but simply that they are not the game's most appealing elements.

The excitement of batting is to dominate the opposition against the odds, and it is the most difficult facet of the game in which to excel because a bowler, wicket-keeper and nine fieldsmen are constantly plotting one player's downfall.

Another aspect of batting which adds to its allure is the *sudden death factor*. No matter how well a batsman is playing, how commanding his stroke play, he can always be out to the next ball, and many wonderful innings have been cut short by the first false stroke made.

By contrast, a bowler has no such qualms. A really bad ball may dispatched for four or six runs but there is always the chance of a comeback with the next ball, if not with another over or spell of bowling later in the day.

The batsman's hope is for good luck and no big innings are played without a measure of it. The uncertain stroke that falls safely in the field, and the ball that beats the bat and misses the off stump by a whisker assist, and sometimes a reprieval comes when a fielder drops a catch. On the other hand, concentration is an essential attribute which must be cultivated in order to achieve high-class performances.

In lower grades of cricket plenty of batsmen have the ability to score regularly in the twenties and thirties but rarely push beyond it. The reason they don't is that they are unable to sustain their *concentration*, and in the first-class game they must do so in order to make regular, worthwhile contributions.

Any batsman who scores moderately well is able to overcome the variations of light and pace of the pitch, and for a time may threaten to overcome the schemes of the attack. But he then frequently suffers a mental lapse and is dismissed.

The good batsman reduces these lapses but he is of little use to his team if he remains immobile at the wicket. The batsman's purpose is to score runs and to do so he must be able to play attacking shots. In addition to defending his stumps he should learn the art of placing the ball through the field and running well between the wickets.

The Strokes

A solid defence is the cornerstone upon which good batting is built.

The *forward defensive stroke* is played against a ball which is well

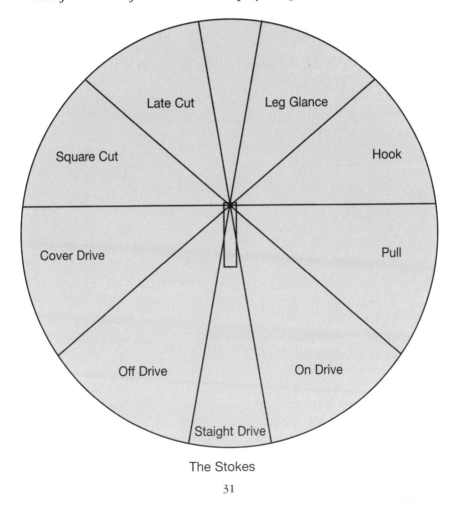

The Stokes

Forward Defensive

pitched up but not far enough to drive. The shot is made with a perpendicular bat, playing the ball close to the front leg so that there is insufficient space for it to pass between bat and pad. The bat is angled well forward at impact.

The *back defensive stroke* is made against a ball pitched short of a length and with a straight bat, the rear foot moving back and across the stumps into a direct line with the oncoming ball, and the front moving across also for balance and as an added protection for the wicket. The bat is angled forward and the left elbow raised at impact.

The drives are aggressive, majestic strokes in front of the wicket and with a full flow of the bat. They may be made off the front or back foot, but the latter are frequently called forcing shots. *Cover, off, straight* and *on drives* are played in response to the direction of the ball delivered.

On Drive

Off Drive

Square Cut

Cut strokes are played with a horizontal bat against deliveries pitched short and outside the off stump. The *square* cut is usually struck off the back foot and square of the wicket while the *back* or *late* cut is a finer deflection between the slips.

The *square drive* is a hybrid stroke, being struck off the front foot and with an oblique bat. It has its on-side equivalent, the *forcing shot off the toes* wide of mid-wicket, which is a combination of a drive with a roll of the wrists.

Pull shots are attacking leg-side strokes made with a cross bat to balls that are short of a length. When playing this shot the batsman is behind the line of the ball and rolls his wrists on impact.

Pull Shot

Hook

Hook strokes are an aggressive counter to short-pitched bowling. The shot is made with a horizontal bat as the batsman moves inside the line of the ball in order to make contact about shoulder height and dispatch it behind square leg. The stroke is hit in the air and carries some element of risk of a catch. Certainly, many fast bowlers prey on a batsmen's liking for the stroke in the hope of dismissing them.

Sweep shots are executed by falling down on the back knee and hitting across the line to place the ball to the square leg boundary, a very profitable shot against off-spin bowlers although more dangerous against leg-spinners if the pitch has a lot of turn and bounce.

Sweep

34

Leg Clance

A *leg glance* is a deflecting stroke produced by rolling the wrists over the ball on contact and placing the ball behind the wicket on the leg side. It can be played off both the front and back foot.

The greatest batsmen not only play all the strokes and concentrate for long periods of time, they also play several strokes of their own invention.

Sir Donald Bradman was said to be unorthodox and played with a cross bat but what he did was reorganise fields by pulling balls just short of a length through the leg side. Some critics thought his tactics in 1932-33 against a new form of attack in Bodyline were flashy but his average of 56.57 was respectable and well ahead of those of his colleagues.

Sir Garfield Sobers is widely regarded as the best all-rounder in the history of the game and when he captained a Rest of the World international side to Australia in 1971-72 he and South African Graeme Pollock, who was also a member of the party, vied for the honour of the world's best batsman. After falling twice to emerging fast bowler Dennis Lillee for no runs in the Second (unofficial) Test at Perth, and again in the first innings of the Third Test in Melbourne, it appeared that his career was on the wane. With successive figures of 8 for 29, 4 for 63 and 5 for 48 Lillee certainly was very much the man of the moment, and when Sobers came to the crease in the second innings in Melbourne he bowled him a fast yorker which would have destroyed the stumps of most batsmen. Instead the great West Indian swayed towards the back foot and crashed the ball down the ground for four runs.

In a flash the balance of play swung back towards the batsman and, although he still had to concentrate while gaining ascendancy, Sobers succeeded, and went on to play an innings of 254 which many judges believed to be the greatest display of batting since the Second World War. For his part Lillee took 3 for 133 and learned a salutary lesson – and one which he remembered on his way to taking 355 Test scalps.

The constant battle between bat and ball is the charm of cricket. If batsmen gain control bowlers counter with new tactics. If a new bowling tactic is proving a constraint a new form of counter must be found by the batsmen.

In recent years batsmen like Sachin Tendulkar, Matthew Hayden and Ricky Ponting have treated bowlers at Test level with disdain. Adam Gilchrist, Brian Lara, Andrew Flintoff and Kevin Pietersen have destroyed them. While Lara's many brilliant innings for the West Indies over the last few years have often been sole hands in lost causes Gilchrist, in a much more powerful batting side, has shown the capacity to change the course of matches in a few overs.

The new cricket watcher can find much to appreciate by coming to understand the checks and balances frequently at work. And a heightened sense of awareness brings a deeper love for the game.

5

A Bowler's Measure

For a long time bowlers were held in poor regard. In England they were once seen as cap-in-hand representatives of a servile class who were paid to bowl to wealthy amateur batsmen and had the status of cricketing cannon-fodder. Later, when first-class cricket became established, they were grudgingly accepted as schemers and plotters whose aim was to bring about another player's downfall.

What is often overlooked, however, is that without great bowlers there can be no great batsmen, and certainly no great contests. In traditional cricket a team may have a powerful batting side but they cannot win a game unless they dismiss their opponents twice for less runs in the time available.

With a ball in his hand the bowler has the initiative. He and his captain set a field, usually with the aim of preying upon a batsman's weakness. Whether the initiative is retained depends upon the bowler's penetration and accuracy. If he has too many tricks for a batsman it is likely that he will dismiss him quickly, but sometimes it is more a war of attrition with a bowler able to restrain but not dismiss a batsman.

A bowler must at all times strive to bowl with good *length and direction*, and to the field that has been set. What is interesting about cricket is that these are variable measures. Bowling a full length to a strong driving batsman can be disastrous but to a back-foot player can prove the correct tactic. Equally, bowling on the line of off stump to one batsman may be best when attacking a leg-side player but ridiculous against one who possesses powerful off-side strokes.

The best bowlers are not, therefore, just those with fine actions, but those who use a number of variations—movement through the air, off the wicket, or a change of pace—to lure the batsman to destruction. Above all the bowler must have the ability to *think* batsmen out.

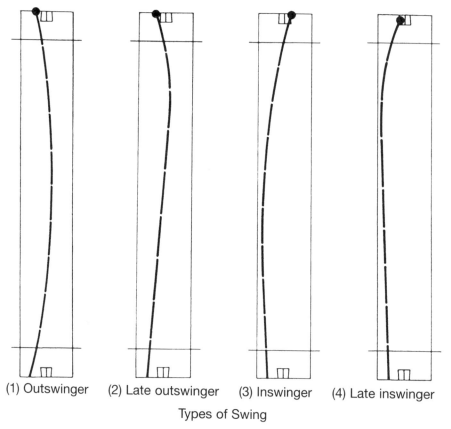

(1) Outswinger (2) Late outswinger (3) Inswinger (4) Late inswinger

Types of Swing

Swing and Swerve

Swing refers to movement through the air caused by the shine on the ball and the direction of the seam. *Swerve* is caused entirely by the spin of the ball as it moves through the air. When a ball swings it usually continues its direction after bouncing but a swerving ball will be likely to spin back the other way. Thus an off-spinner will find he may drift the ball away from the batsman's off stump and a leg-spinner drift outside the leg stump.

The best conditions for swing are with a new ball in a humid atmosphere with a breeze blowing in the right direction. Bowlers polish the ball keeping the shine on one side in order to make it swing as long as possible.

The outswinger, which moves through the air with the shiny side of the ball leading from the leg to the off side and leaves the batsman, is delivered with the seam of the ball pointing towards the slips and with the bowling arm slightly roundarm.

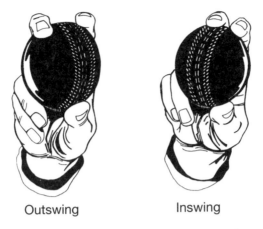

Outswing   Inswing

The *inswinger*, which moves into the batsman through the air from the off to the leg side, is delivered with the seam of the ball pointing towards fine leg and the bowling action as high as possible.

Swing bowling aims to defeat the batsmen by virtue of its movement but the ball which bends early in flight is by no means as dangerous as that which moves late and puts the batsman in danger of being bowled, trapped lbw or giving a catch close to the wicket.

The most favourable winds for swing bowling are light breezes which blow from third slip for inswingers and from fine leg for outwsingers.

Reverse swing is achieved with an old ball. By turning it through 180 degrees and swapping the shiny and rough sides an outswinger can be delivered with an inswing technique and seam angle. Pioneered by Pakistani pace bowler Sarfraz Nawaz in the mid-1980s it was perfected by his countrymen Wasim Akram and Waqar Younis in the 1990s, and used to great effect by Englishmen Andrew Flintoff and Simon Jones in the 2005 Ashes Series.

Cut and Seam

Cut is a term used to describe two types of deliveries which pace bowlers employ in extracting movement off the wicket. Cut is like quick spin and is achieved by the bowler cutting his fingers down one or the other side of the ball.

An *off cutter* comes into a batsman and is likely to bowl him or trap him lbw whereas a *leg cutter* is a ball which moves away to the slips and is usually attempted in an effort to bring about a dismissal with a catch behind the wicket.

Seam is achieved by holding the ball lightly with the seam upright and with the object of landing it on the seam and causing it to deviate one way or the other. The trick is that if the bowler has no idea which way it will move the batsmen will have even less idea.

Off Break

Spin

Spin refers to movement off the pitch caused by bowlers spinning the fingers, wrists or combinations of both. Off and leg spin are the most common varieties. *Off spin* (or the *off break*) is a ball which comes into the batsman after hitting the pitch, and it is easy to bowl as it is achieved with a natural swing of the arm. The spin is obtained from the action of the index finger turning the ball in a clockwise direction with a simultaneous twist of the wrist.

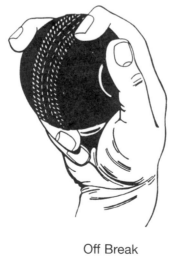

Off Break

Leg Break

Off breaks are usually delivered from a high hand position and may be bowled with great accuracy. They are an extremely dangerous proposition when a pitch begins to wear.

For variation off-spinners usually bowl an arm ball which when swerving away from the batsman goes on with the arm and since the 1990s a number of off-spinners from Sri Lanka, Pakistan and India have

Leg Break

experimented with a new delivery, the *doosra*, which is delivered with an off-break action but which spins from the leg.

Leg spin (or the *leg break*) is a ball which pitches on the leg side and moves towards the off side. The spin is given by the third finger combined with wrist action, and the ball rotates anti-clockwise in flight.

The top spinner is delivered with a similar action to the leg break but slightly earlier. It has little or no turn and gathers pace from the pitch. The *flipper* is a type of top-spinner.

The *googly* (sometimes called a *bosey* or a *wrong'un*) is the master deception practiced by leg-spinners. It is a ball delivered slightly later than the leg break, with the back of the hand facing the batsman so that on pitching it breaks from the off instead of the leg.

| (1) Underarm | (2) Roundarm | (3) Overarm |

Evolution of Bowling

If the reader is not becoming too confused at this point perhaps the expressions *orthodox* and *unorthodox spinner* will do the job. These terms apply only to left-arm spin bowlers whereas there is no comparable term governing left-arm fast bowlers. An *orthodox spinner* is a left-arm finger spinner whose natural delivery turns away from the leg to the off side and is thus a left-arm leg-spinner. An *unorthodox spinner* is a left-arm wrist spinner whose main delivery turns from the off side to the leg. If an unorthodox spinner can bowl a googly this really creates argument. Whereas in England this ball which spun away from the bat was often described as a *Chinaman* it used to be the opposite ball – the one spinning into the batsman – which was so described in Australia. Unfortunately, even among Australians who think of themselves of cricket experts, the definition now seems to be inclining towards the English view.

Bowling Styles

All types of bowling have had their day. *Underarm* or *lob bowling* was used exclusively until the 1820s. This form enabled bowlers to achieve a high degree of spin and swerve but gave way to *roundarm* when batsmen began to dominate play. This method of bowling was much faster and the ball moved away from the batsman. However, it lacked the subtleties and variations which came with the introduction of overarm bowling.

In the nineteenth century the great bowlers either spun or cut the ball from the off, or were left-arm spinners who turned the ball from the leg. As wickets became more level and bounce more even, faster bowlers such as England's Tom Richardson and Australia's Ernest Jones appeared as potent strike weapons, while Bernard Bosanquet revolutionised the craft of right-arm leg-spinners around 1900 with the invention of the googly.

Over the years it has chiefly been the bowlers who have had to develop new strategies in order to keep on level pegging with the batsmen. They have often been driven to invention by batsmen using pads for the protection of their stumps rather than their legs.

Sometimes the game's lawmakers stepped in with some assistance. In 1946 in England, for instance, an experimental law was permitted whereby a new ball was introduced every 55 overs. Although this law only lasted for a few years, the reason for its introduction was that there were fears that fast bowling was dying out.

This certainly may have appeared true because in the period between the First and Second World Wars Australia's Ted McDonald and Jack Gregory, England's Harold Larwood, and West Indians' Learie Constantine and 'Manny' Martindale were the only really fast bowlers operating in international cricket, with Larwood the fastest of the group.

Ray Lindwall and Keith Miller were the second great Australian fast bowling combination, and they spearheaded the attack when Test cricket resumed after the Second World War. Then nobody else bowled at express pace until Dennis Lillee came on the scene in 1970. For England, Frank Tyson was nicknamed 'Typhoon' because of his explosive speed in the 1950s, and West Indians' Wesley Hall and Charlie Griffith bowled at frightening speed during the mid-1960s.

In the 1980s the dominant attacks were based on speed and since 1976 the West Indian selection of four fast bowlers revolutionised previous thinking about cricket to such an extent that in their dominance of the game until 1995 spin bowling came to be in danger of becoming obsolete.

Why one form of bowling becomes more popular than another at any given time relates to role models and the nature of wickets. Quick, bouncy wickets in Perth produced a succession of fine fast medium bowlers for Western Australia in Sheffield Shield cricket, the greatest of whom, Graham McKenzie, was an outstanding opening bowler for Australia in the 1960s. McKenzie was, therefore, a likely model for a young Dennis Lillee, and Lillee (and Jeff Thomson) have no doubt inspired the generation of bowlers to follow such as Rodney Hogg, Geoff Lawson, Craig McDermott, Merv Hughes, Glenn McGrath and Jason Gillespie.

In the West Indies, Hall and Griffith were the start of a production line of fearsome fast bowlers which included Andy Roberts, Michael Holding, Joel Garner, Colin Croft, Malcolm Marshall, Curtley Ambrose, Ian Bishop and Courtney Walsh.

The role models then began to extend internationally and even countries such as Pakistan and India, which in the past produced deadly slow wickets suitable only for spinners and medium pacers found fast and penetrative opening bowlers in Imran Khan, Wasim Akram, Waqar Younis, Shoaib Akhtar, Kapil Dev and Jarvagal Srinath.

Watching a very fast bowler such as Shoaib or Brett Lee can be one of the most exhilarating sights in cricket. But many bowlers simply run a long way giving an illusion of speed until they let the ball go. The result was that in the 1980s with less overs being bowled and the ball frequently being pitched short of a length the batsman had little opportunity to exercise his strokes. There was also a sameness about the play which was likely to dull the cricket watcher's enthusiasm.

Although spin bowling remained alive in India, spinners in other countries often bowled in a negative manner while the pace men rested.

The only attacking leg-spinner in the game was Pakistani Abdul Qadir. Then came Shane Warne.

The Australian summer of 1991-92 first saw the appearance of Warne in the Test side as a 22-year-old but, although he took a hiding from India's Ravi Shastri in his first match, within two years he was a champion and a dominant influence in the modern game. A lot of young boys might have started flicking their fingers and wrists in front of television sets in imitation of Warne yet while only Stuart MacGill (seventeen months younger than Warne) has prospered for Australia a lot of inventive spinners have appeared elsewhere. Sri Lanka's Muttiah Muralitharan, India's Anil Kumble and Harbahjan Singh, Pakistan's Mushtaq Ahmed, Saqlain Mushtaq and Danish Kaneria, South Africa's Paul Adams, and New Zealand's Daniel Vettori have all kept spin alive.

The game of cricket is best when it is balanced, and a bowling attack comprising the elements of speed, swing and spin is far more engaging to watch than one which consists of a number of bowlers of similar type.

6

Fielding —The Third Discipline

All the main batting strokes as we now know them have been played since what was known as the Golden Age of cricket ended in 1914. All the forms of bowling had been invented by that time. The biggest advance in the game has been the improvement in fielding standards and most of this improvement has been in the last thirty years.

Fielders may be the pawns in the game but they are very important pawns, particularly in the psychological warfare waged between batsmen and bowlers.

There have always been great fielders: Jack Gregory, Wally Hammond and Bob Simpson at slip; Learie Constantine anywhere; Vic Richardson at point; Gary Sobers and Tony Lock at short leg; a succession of cover fieldsman from Jack Hobbs to Neil Harvey, South African Colin Bland, and (in his early years) Clive Lloyd. But most sides contained several men they had to hide in the field because of their slowness or the weakness of their throwing arms.

In the modern era, however, first-class cricketers have paid greater attention to fitness and catching practice. The result has been that what were often merely half chances are now accepted as catches, and many more drives are cut off by acrobatic dives and boundaries reduced by fielders sliding along the turf and hooking the ball into play. A more recent practice has been for outfielders to chase balls to the boundary in pairs and for the first to flick the ball back to a partner who then rapidly relays it to the wicket-keeper or bowler's wicket.

Attacking fielding

As many matches are lost or won because of the fielding as they are because of the strength of the batting or bowling. Batsmen are certainly demoralised by a fielding side which through agility, alertness and anticipation, brings about dismissals by brilliant catching, by safe and

46

Pick up on the run

clean pick-ups which prevent or reduce runs from aggressive strokes, and by fast, accurate returns which effect run outs.

Bowlers, on the hand, are likely to be boosted by such efforts and inspired to greater performances.

The attacking fielder acts with a sense of urgency and players such as Englishman Derek Randall, the West Indian Roger Harper and South African Jonty Rhodes were inspirational figures in their sides. The attacking fielder runs as quickly as he can to intercept a ball, and even if another fielder stops it he runs behind him to back up.

Most fielders in the close-catching positions have superb reflexes and none more so than Mark Waugh at second slip where he made many wonderful catches throughout his career. At short leg David Boon became a superb fielder in the 1980s and 1990s after intense drilling by Australian coach Bob Simpson. Seldom do the players in these positions see more than the blur of a ball coming to them.

Often the close fielder's presence is intimidatory. Former England captain Tony Greig often stood extremely close to the bat at silly point, his 200 cm frame towering over the batsman. Greig aimed to menace the batsman out by causing him to play a tentative stroke.

Defensive Fielding

The object of defensive fielding is to reduce run scoring, and the fielder watches each delivery by the bowler and the movement of the batsman's feet in order to assess the direction of the stroke.

Body behind the ball

The cricket watcher will notice that outfielders begin to walk towards the wicket as the bowler approaches his delivery. They do this so that they are already moving and it is easier for them to move to a ball which has been hit. What will not be so readily apparent is that the ball rarely travels in a straight line. Off-side strokes are sliced and will move from right to left as the ball approaches while on-side strokes veer from left to right.

In stopping most balls the fielder will use two hands and gather the ball near his right foot in order to move his left foot forward and get the

The Return

most power into his throw. On occasions though, when stopping a hard drive, the fielder will place more of his body behind the ball so that he will reduce the chances of misfielding and of the ball slipping through his fingers and going to the boundary.

Good outfielding requires cricketers to maintain their concentration even if they have more time to react to strokes than close to the wicket fielders. Most batsmen are out to catches, many of which come from mistimed drives. An outfielder who is quick off the mark may make valuable metres to a catch which would otherwise have fallen safely to the ground. Similarly, an early movement towards the ball frequently cuts down the value of scoring shots from threes to twos, and twos to singles, factors which may be important in the final analysis.

Wicket-keeping

Wicket-keeping is the most demanding job in cricket, for while there are eleven batsmen in a team and a bowling attack consisting of four or five players, there is only one wicket-keeper who must concentrate intently on every ball during an innings.

The wicket-keeper is a close fielder with a lot of extra responsibilities, and he wears gloves and pads for his protection. Like other close fielders he must be ready to move quickly in any direction and thus crouches near the ground as the bowler runs in to bowl.

From this position he can move quickly from one side to the other, diving for catches or to stop a wide ball, or springing into the air to take a high catch or stop a bouncer.

If the ball is allowed to pass or beats the bat the wicket-keeper must gauge its direction and take the ball in his gloves. At other times he must be alert to the chance of catches and stumpings. If the batsman plays a stroke and runs the wicket-keeper has to take position behind the stumps to receive return throws from the field.

Wicket-keepers receive the ball standing back to fast and medium-fast bowlers with the aim of taking the ball about waist high, and stand up to the wicket for slow bowlers. This is partly good sense and partly a trend. The modern idea puts safety first, as it is claimed that fewer catches are missed by the man standing back. But in earlier days the wicket-keepers created chances by stumping from fast bowlers, and indeed were often referred to as stumpers. A spectacular dismissal made in this way in modern times was English wicket-keeper Jack Russell's leg-side stumping of Dean Jones from the bowling of Gladstone Small at the Sydney Cricket Ground in 1991. Generally, however, the term has little meaning as few stumpings are made even from spin bowlers.

To give some indication of how the role of wicket-keeping has changed it is worth noting that Australia's first gloveman Jack Blackham made 36 catches and 24 stumpings in 35 Tests and interwar keeper Bert Oldfield made 78 catches and 52 stumpings in 54 Tests. By contrast Rod Marsh made only 12 stumpings against 343 catches in his 97 game career. Marsh, of course, played in an era dominated by pace bowlers and at the time fellow keepers such as Englishmen Alan Knott and Bob Taylor, and West Indians' Derryck Murray and Jeff Dujon feasted off the fast men, and their tumbling catches became features of the age. In Australia, although Ian Healy and Adam Gilchrist have had the benefit of keeping wickets to Shane Warne and Stuart MacGill the percentage of victims falling to stumpings has been small.

Wicket-keeper (crouching)

Receiving the ball

7

Talking Tactics

How a particular game of cricket is played depends upon a number of factors such as the state of the wicket, whether the two teams are involved in a series of matches or a knockout situation, the composition of the teams, and the personalities of the captains. While captains exercise a certain amount of free will in making decisions they are frequently made within a predetermined frame of reference.

If a captain wins the toss and decides to bat he should lay down a policy for his team and some clues should be provided by his opening batsmen. If they score freely it may be that they are seizing the initiative from the bowlers, that the pitch is playing easily, or that there are few threats from the attack. On the other hand, if the openers are playing defensively it may be that they lack imagination, that the pitch is difficult, or that the bowlers are in control.

Much of the way cricket is played is mental. Some players like Matthew Hayden in recent years have looked to dominate from the outset while other opening batsmen have adopted a defensive approach. At one time it used to be said that the bowler bowled as well as he was allowed to by the batsmen, but the emphasis often alters so that control is said to be in the hand of the bowler. When West Indian opening batsmen Sherwin Campbell and Daren Ganga failed to score in their first seven overs against Glenn McGrath and Jason Gillespie at the Melbourne Cricket Ground in 2000 the bowlers were definitely in control.

Part of the reason for a defensive attitude is that national sides have sometimes been more afraid of losing than they are keen to win, and the drawn game is a haven for those for whom caution is a byword. This charge certainly could not be levelled against Australian sides in the Steve Waugh era.

A remarkable facet of cricket is often how quickly fortunes change with the arrival of a new batsman. Sometimes a bowler who has been on top of the batting is struck for a couple of fours and the balance of the game changes. At other times two batsmen have made a big partnership and seem to have the attack on its knees, then one is dismissed and all of a sudden the initiative may swing back to the bowling side.

Attack or defence is easy to see when practised by batsmen but less apparent when practised by the fielding side.

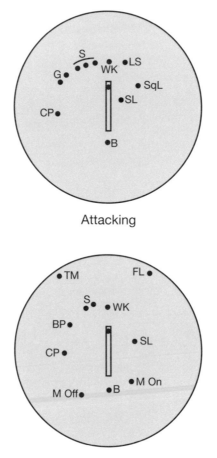

Attacking

Defensive Fast Bowling

At the start of an innings most fast bowlers with a new ball are given an attacking field. This may consist of three slips and two gullies and three men close to the wicket on the leg side. Such an arrangement is called an *umbrella field* and frequently only one man in the covers is forward of the wicket on the off-side. The batsman is therefore surrounded by fielders, but if he uses a little enterprise and strokes the ball firmly there are plenty of gaps in the field and the chance to pick up quick runs. The fielding captain is aware of this risk but may be prepared to sacrifice a few runs for the chance of a wicket.

If the batsmen are playing defensively the attacking field may be maintained for longer. If the score is mounting rapidly the captain may start removing his slips and short legs to place fielders at third man and fine leg. Later he may also strengthen the covers and mid-wicket area. A fast bowler in such circumstances would be said to be operating to a defensive field.

At these times a captain needs to be sensitive to his bowlers. He must have confidence in his men but not be foolhardy. If a batsman hits an off-drive for four and the captain's immediate reaction is to take one of the slips away and put a mid-off in position he may be destroying the bowler's plan for a catch and cause resentment. On the other hand, if the batsman is gaining the ascendancy he may replace his bowler, or block the batsman's run scoring opportunities.

An interesting poser is now set for the batsman. His task is to upset the rearranged bowling plans. If the field is relatively close to the bat the occasional lofted stroke into the outfield may help break it up, while if it is set deeper batsmen must be on the lookout for quickly run singles. The batsman who attempts to loft the ball takes a risk of being caught out if he mistimes his shot, but a player who simply occupies the crease and waits for a bad ball to hit may not take advantage of it when it comes.

Bowlers, of course, operate to different fields with varying intentions, and a field described as defensive for a fast bowler can be attacking for an off-spinner. For example, the latter may have one slip, two short legs,

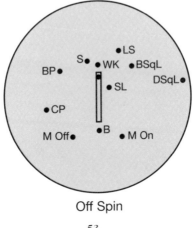

Off Spin

and the rest of the fielders away from the bat, including a deep mid-wicket in a catching position. With such a field he can be bowling aggressively whereas a pace bowler with the same field could be accused of negative tactics.

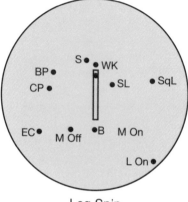

Leg Spin

Another variation of field for a leg-spinner could include a slip, silly mid-off, and a short leg, but no other fielder near the bat, yet a deep extra cover could be strategically placed to catch a misdirected drive.

There are many ways of dismissing batsmen, and trapping them on their strengths can sometimes prove as effective as preying on a weakness. For this reason fast bowlers frequently bowl bumpers to have batsmen play a favourite hook shot too early or too often. The result might then be a catch on the fine leg boundary, another example of a deep-set position being used for an attacking purpose.

One consideration which always causes a lot of discussion is the action of a captain winning the toss and sending his opponents in to bat. At one time such an action used to be construed as meaning that a captain believed a pitch to be lively, and was seeking to let his pace bowlers take advantage of it. The disadvantage was always that the side then had to bat last on a wearing pitch.

In the 1980s and 1990s the move was viewed more defensively particularly when facing the power of the West Indies' pace attack. In such circumstances opposing captains were not thinking about the advantages for their bowlers but the disadvantages to their batsmen and the prospect of being dismissed for a low score. Since the West Indies invariably used a four-man pace attack without a front-line spinner batting in a fourth innings did not hold the perils it might have under other conditions, and therefore such a decision made good sense.

In recent years sides have sometimes made similar decisions against Australia. However, their attacks have then been exposed to Australia's strong batting in the best conditions. And while they avoided a potent trio of fast bowlers they have then had to deal with Shane Warne on a turning wicket at the end of a game.

A problem which is sometimes perplexing, is deciding whether to enforce a follow-on when a side is more than 200 runs behind on a first innings in a Test match, although again the prospect of possibly having to use tired bowlers, and batting in the last innings of a match has caused some sides to pass up the opportunity.

Australia's phenomenal 16 Test match winning streak ended at Kolkata in 2001 when the Australians led India by 274 runs (445 to 171) on the first innings and Steve Waugh put the Indians in again. At 3-115 the Australians appeared well on top and at 4-232 still held an advantage but a superb fighting partnership of 376 by V.V.S. Laxman and Rahul Dravid saw off defeat and opened a winning opportunity which off-spinner Harbahjan Singh took as Australia was bundled out for 212 to lose the game by 171 runs.

Although it was a freak turnaround, and although Australia has remained top dog in world cricket, the memory of that defeat has remained so that the Australians have remained notably cautious about enforcing follow-ons in recent times.

Under Ricky Ponting, at home, in the 2004-05 season Australia had easy wins in successive matches over New Zealand in the Second Test at Adelaide, and Pakistan in the First Test in Perth. Yet the wins could have been easier. Certainly, quicker. In neither was the follow-on applied. In Adelaide the Australians led by 324 runs on the first innings (8-575 to 251) and ran to a lead of 463 runs before declaring and leaving his side around ten hours to dismiss his opponents. As it turned out Ponting's decision probably pleased cricket administrators as the match dragged on until after lunch on the fifth day but the overall 213 margin probably flattered the New Zealanders.

In the second game, however, the 491 run win might be viewed as farcical by making a four day game of one which should only have lasted three. After Australia had made 381 runs in its first innings Pakistan was dismissed for 179 and the follow-on could have been enforced. That it was not when the bowlers had delivered only 77.3 overs was strange and watchers were then left with the strange spectacle of the Australians piling up a meaningless 5-361 runs in their second innings to lead by 563 runs before a declaration was made. That Pakistan was then put out for

72 in less than two and a half hours, was lamentable, and a psychological blow, but cricket watchers would be left wondering whether the end justified the means.

When to change bowlers may be another awkward tactical decision. Some bowlers thrive on hard work and others need to be nursed along in shorter spells. In limited over matches a captain may be tempted to bowl his best bowler right through his ten overs, or save some of his overs to the end of the innings when the batting side is throwing the bat around. This is not a simple matter because while the bowler might have a restraining influence later, he might also lose his early rhythm and be punished severely.

At other times bowlers may be changed because a new batsman plays one type of bowling less confidently than another. The best tactic in such cases is introduce the type he least favours into the attack even if it means removing the bowler who took a wicket. Sometimes even accomplished batsmen become the 'rabbit' of a particular bowler and a thoughtful captain exploits such opportunities.

The timing of declarations depends on many things. The state of the wicket, the ability of the bowlers, the batting strength of the opposition, and the relative positions of the two teams in a competition or series. When to declare is never an easy matter for judgement but caution often overrides enterprise. For a game in which heavy store is placed on statistics favourable odds have often been overlooked by safety-first captains.

For example, only three times in Test cricket history has a side won a match by scoring over 400 runs in the fourth innings: by the West Indies against Australia at St. John's, Antigua in 2003; India against the West Indies at Port-of-Spain in 1975-76; and Australia against England at Leeds in 1948. Indeed, totals of over 300 are rare, yet West Indian captain Clive Lloyd, with eleven consecutive Test wins behind him and a 3-nil lead in the 1984-85 series, delayed his declaration in the Fourth Test against Australia in Melbourne until the final morning of the match. At that point his team led by 369 runs with only about five hours for play.

Perhaps Lloyd put too much faith in his bowlers being able to dismiss Australia easily as they had done in earlier matches. But if that was the case why had he set such a high victory target. Perhaps he remembered that he had been on the receiving end at Portof-Spain. But his tactics cost him dearly. Australia struggled to end the day at 8-198 but escaped with a draw and the chance to breathe easily. Not only did Lloyd miss the chance to beat Australia 5-nil for the first time in history, but a revived

Australian side turned the tables on him in the last Test and Lloyd ended his career with an innings defeat.

A far more sensible declaration was made by Adam Gilchrist as stand-in captain for Steve Waugh at Headingley in 2001. With Australia leading the series 3-nil it had scored 447 in its first innings to lead England by 138 and made a quick-fire 4-176 in its second innings before declaring just before stumps on the fourth day with a lead of 314 runs against a powerful attack of Glenn McGrath, Jason Gillespie, Brett Lee and Shane Warne. Gilchrist had the numbers in his favour but what he did not account for was the superb innings played by Mark Butcher whose 173 not out was the exact same score as Don Bradman made on the same ground in Australia's win fifty-three years earlier. While a surprising amount of criticism was levelled at Gilchrist it can well be argued that most of his critics were being wise after the event.

The discerning cricket watcher would have supported Gilchrist's move. He or she should also try to imagine what thoughts are occupying the minds of batsmen, bowlers and captains. Trying to work out one's own solutions is akin to detective work and one of the fascinations of the game.

8

The Umpires' Rules

Cricket matches are played under the control of two umpires who are required by the Laws of the Game to be 'absolutely impartial'.

The umpires have numerous duties before a match begins. Much of this involves inspecting the condition of the pitch, meeting the captains and scorers, checking team lists, and wicket alignment, and supervising the toss for the choice of innings. The umpires walk to the pitch five minutes before the scheduled starting time and agree upon a choice of ends.

On the field the umpires stand in two positions. One is at the striker's end and square of the wicket so as to have a view of it and the batsman's feet at right angles. He is called the square leg umpire because he usually stands in that position, but he may stand on the other side of the wicket at point. The other umpire stands at the bowler's end in a direct line behind the wicket and looking at the striker's wicket. As the bowling attack switches ends at the completion of an over the umpires reverse roles by moving to the wicket at the bowling end and away from it square of the wicket.

During play umpires have enormous responsibilities but the most important involve answering appeals and giving signals to scorers. The *bowling end umpire* answers appeals for bowled, caught, handled the ball, hit the ball twice, lbw, obstructing the field, and timed out. He also calls and signals 'no-ball' (chiefly for the bowler infringing with his feet), 'wide ball' and calls 'over' at the end of the required number of balls. The *square leg umpire* answers appeals of hit wicket, and stumped, and is the more likely to call and signal 'no-ball' for throwing if he doubts the fairness of a bowler's action. He watches the batsmen to see whether they have crossed when a ball may be caught or there is the prospect of a run out. *Both umpires* answer appeals for run outs at their end, call and signal short runs and dead balls where applicable, count balls per over, and assist their colleague at all times.

The Signals

Out

Out
In Chapter 2 we examined the ten ways of being dismissed. To show that a batsman is out the umpire raises the index finger of one hand above his head. If the umpire is denying the appeal he shall call 'not out'.

Bye

Bye
When a ball passes the striker without touching him or his bat and any runs are obtained, these are recorded as byes unless such a ball is first called a 'wide' or 'no-ball'.

The umpire signals a bye by raising an open hand above his head.

Leg Bye

Leg bye
If runs are taken from a ball which strikes the body or playing apparel of a batsman while he is endeavouring to make a stroke they are recorded as leg byes.

The umpire signals a leg bye by raising one knee and touching it with his hand.

Wide

Wide

When a bowler bowls a ball which is so wide of the wicket or flies so high over the batsman's head that he cannot reach it in making a stroke it is called a 'wide ball' with one qualification—that there is a stricter interpretation of wides in limited over matches than in other games.

The umpire calls 'wide ball' and signals wide by extending both arms horizontally.

No-ball

No-ball

The most common call of '*no-ball*' is made when a bowler places his front foot over the popping crease, or when his back foot lands on or outside the return crease.

The most controversial call is when an umpire believes a bowler is throwing the ball by bending and straightening his arm in the delivery action.

Other actions which will bring a call of 'no-ball' include:

(1) A bowler throwing the ball at the striker's wicket in an effort to run him out before bowling at him.

(2) A bowler delivering a ball which bounces more than twice or rolls along the ground.

(3) More than two fielders are stationed behind the popping crease on the leg side.

(4) Any part of a fielder's body extends onto the pitch prior to the batsman playing the ball.

(5) The wicket-keeper moves in front of the wicket before a ball has been hit by or touched the striker, passes the wicket, or the striker attempts to run.

(6) If a bowler is delivering fast short-pitched balls in a dangerous or unfair manner.

(7) If a bowler is delivering high full-pitched balls in a dangerous or unfair manner.

The umpires signals no-ball by raising one arm horizontally.

Boundary Four   Boundary Six

Boundaries

A stroke which runs over the boundary line after bouncing is awarded *four runs* and is signalled by the umpire waving one arm from side to side. *Six runs* is awarded when a ball is struck over the boundary on the full. This is signalled by the umpire raising both hands in the air.

Dead ball

There are many instances in a game when the ball is dead but thankfully not all these need to be signalled.

One which does occurs when batsmen attempt to run a leg bye from a deflection but no stroke has been made and the batsman has not been trying to avoid being struck by the ball.

Dead Ball

Other occasions which require signalling are:

(1) Intervention in dealing with unfair play.

(2) When a player is seriously injured.

(3) When the striker is not ready to receive the ball.

(4) If the bowler drops the ball before delivery or fails to let go of it.

(5) The bails fall from the striker's wicket prior to delivery.

(6) An umpire leaves his position for consultation.

An umpire signals dead ball by crossing and recrossing his wrists below the waist.

Penalty runs
An umpire signals five penalty runs to the batting side by repeatedly tapping one shoulder with the opposite hand.

Penalty run

New ball
The bowler's end umpire signals new ball by holding the ball above his head.

New ball

Revoke last signal
An umpire signals by touching both shoulders each with the opposite hand.

Revoke last
signal

Short run

If a batsman does not run or at least ground his bat from one popping crease to the other while running between the wickets the umpire should signal one run short after he and his partner have finished running. That run shall then be deducted from the number the pair ran.

The umpire signals a *short run* by bending one arm upwards and touching the nearer shoulder with the finger tips.

One short

Third Umpire

In Australia the third umpires are appointed by Cricket Australia and must be members of the International Cricket Council Elite or Cricket Australia National Panels.

The third umpire acts as an emergency and umpire and officiates with regard to TV replays in all televised matches where the technology is available. The third umpire will only officiate when the umpires on the field have referred a decision to him.

Either the on-field or third umpire may call for a TV replay to assist in making a decision about whether a fielder has any part of his person in contact with the ball when he touched or crossed a boundary line or whether a four or six has been scored.

9

Keeping Score

Cricket is a statistician's delight. Originally runs were recorded by carving notches in a piece of wood but scoring is now much more sophisticated.

Every ball a bowler now delivers is recorded (by means of a dot) as is every run that a batsman scores.

A run is made whenever batsmen run between the wickets. If the ball is hit further away from the fielder they may run twice and score two runs, and sometimes for strokes that are a long way from the field, three or four runs.

Four runs are added when the ball goes over the boundary line after bouncing first, and six if it goes over on the full. Occasionally batsmen may run five before the ball reaches the boundary in which case five runs is awarded for the stroke.

Sometimes batsmen receive an unexpected bonus in the form of overthrows. This occurs following a wild return or the fielder throws the ball at the wicket in attempting a run out and no one is backing up behind. Former New South Wales captain Barry Rothwell in the 1960s once scored eight runs from a single stroke in a Sheffield Shield match when he had run four, and a fielder's overthrow went to the boundary and gave him another four runs.

The scorer not only records the mounting totals of individual batsmen but the number of boundaries they hit, the number of balls they receive, how they are out, and the amount of time they were batting before being dismissed. In addition, there is the team score which is checked off and the total recorded when wickets fall. This system of credits also has it balance, however, in debiting runs against the bowlers' analyses. There details of overs bowled, wickets taken and run free overs (known as maidens) are also kept.

In addition, extras as awarded by the umpires are recorded but while byes and leg byes are not debited against the bowlers' figures wides and no-balls are.

An oddity is the awarding of five penalty runs when a fielder stops the ball by a means other than with some part of his body. The penalty runs are then awarded to the batsman if he struck the ball, but otherwise to extras. An example would be a fielder throwing his cap on the ball to slow it down.

There are a couple of cases when runs are not counted but concern those taken before a batsman is out. If a batsman hits a high ball and takes a run but is then caught, the run is disallowed. On the other hand, if a batsman is run out, the run in question is not allowed but any taken beforehand are.

At the completion of an innings there is a three-way check on the score, the totals of batsmen plus extras balancing the total team score, and the runs taken from the bowlers plus the byes and leg byes.

AUSTRALIAN CRICKET BOARD

LUNCH SCORES

TEA SCORES

STUMPS SCORES

MATCH __SOUTH AUSTRALIA__ v __WESTERN AUSTRALIA__.

AT __ADELAIDE OVAL__ ON __26-29 JANUARY, 1990__.

__1ST__ INNINGS OF __WESTERN AUSTRALIA__ DATE __27·1·90__

UMPIRES M.D. O'CONNELL   NORTH END   D.P. REBECK SOUTH END

CAPTAINS D.W. HOOKES(SA)   G.M. WOOD (WA)

WICKET-KEEPERS D.S. BERRY (SA)   T.J. ZOEHRER (WA)

12th MEN M.C. REYAN (SA)   R.S. RUSSELL (WA)

TOSS WON BY   G.M. WOOD

TEAM BATTING FIRST   SOUTH AUSTRALIA

SCORERS R.H. ARTIS   T. LOWREY

	BATSMEN		TIME IN	TIME OUT	MINS	50	100	RUNS AS SCORED	HOW OUT	BOWLER	RUNS	BALLS	4's	6's
1	McPHEE	M.W	3·34	4·38	64			11422 —	BOWLED	SCUDERI	10	40	1	·
2	VELETTA	M.R.J	3·34	4·17	43			1112142 —	C MILLER	GEORGE	13	40	1	·
3	MOODY	T.M.	4·18	4·53	35			114 —	BOWLED	SCUDERI	6	27	1	·
4	WOOD	G.M.	4·39	4·47	8			11 —	C BERRY	MILLER	2	7	·	·
5	ANDREWS	W.S	4·48	4·56	8			1 —	L.B.W	MILLER	0	3	·	·
6	ZOEHRER	T.J.	4·54	5·04	10			—	L.B.W	SCUDERI	0	1	·	·
7	HOGAN	T.G.	4·57	5·10	13			11 —	C BERRY	MILLER	2	13	·	·
8	MATHEWS	C.D	5·05	5·15	10			1 —	BOWLED	SCUDERI	0	5	·	·
9	CAPES	P.A	5·11	5·24	13			—	C BERRY	SCUDERI	1	9	·	·
10	ALDERMAN	T.M	5·16	5·17	1			—	C BERRY	SCUDERI	0	2	·	·
11	YARDLEY	B.	5·18	5·24	6			—	NOT	OUT	0	0	·	·

RUNS TIME	MINS	OVER	BYES 23	LEG-BYES	WIDES	NO BALLS 2	TOTAL SUNDRIES 7			TOTAL
			1	2	3	4	5	6	7	

FALL OF WICKET	1	2	3	4	5	6	7	8	9	10	TOTAL
BATSMAN OUT	VELETTA	McPHEE	WOOD	MOODY	ANDREWS	ZOEHRER	HOGAN	MATHEWS	CAPES	YARDLEY O	41
BATSMAN N.O.	McPHEE	MOODY 2	MOODY 2	ANDREWS O	ZOEHRER O	HOGAN 2	MATHEWS O	CAPES O	ALDERMAN	CAPES	
PARTNERSHIP	23	6	5	4	O	2	O	O	O	O	
BALLS	67	31	10	11	7	9	6	5	2	8	
HOURS	1	2	3								
OVERS	15										
RUNS	29										

| | 50 | 100 | 150 | 200 | 250 | 300 | 350 | 400 | 450 | 500 | 550 |

NR OF OVERS AT START OF COMPULSORY PERIOD

NR OF OVERS TO BE BOWLED IN COMPULSORY PERIOD

POINTS:— HOME TEAM   :VISITING TEAM

RESULT

AWARD:—

INNINGS TIME 110 MINS

1ST. INNINGS OF SOUTH AUSTRALIA v WESTERN AUSTRALIA — BOWLING ANALYSIS

BOWLER	OVERS	MDNS	RUNS	WKTS
GEORGE S.P.	8	2	16	1
MILLER C.R.	12	4	14	3
SCUDERI J.C.	4.2	1	6	6
B, LB/RO			5	
TOTAL	24.2	7	41	10

	SCORE OFF	OVER TO	SCORE ON	OVER FROM	END	TIME ON
GEORGE S.P.	29	15	·	1	N	3.34
MILLER C.R.	41	24	2	2	5	3.38
SCUDERI J.C.	41	24½	29	17	N	4.36

England v Australia 2005 (1st Test)

21,22,23,24 July, 2005. Lord's, London.

Toss: Australia   Result: Australia won by 239 runs

AUSTRALIA

J.L. Langer	c Harmison b Flintoff	40
M.L. Hayden	b Hoggard	12
*R.T. Ponting	c Strauss b Harmison	9
D.R. Martyn	c G.Jones b S.Jones	2
M.J. Clarke	lbw b S.Jones	11
S.M. Katich	c G.Jones b Harmison	27
#A.C. Gilchrist	c G.Jones b Flintoff	26
S.K. Warne	b Harmison	28
B. Lee	c G.Jones b Harmison	3
J.W. Gillespie	lbw b Harmison	1
G.D. McGrath	not out	10
Extras	(B 5, LB 4, W 1, NB 11)	21
TOTAL		190

J.L. Langer	run out	6
M.L. Hayden	b Flintoff	34
*R.T. Ponting	c sub (Hildreth) b Hoggard	42
D.R. Martyn	lbw b Harmison	65
M.J. Clarke	b Hoggard	91
S.M. Katich	c S.Jones b Harmison	67
#A.C. Gilchrist	b Flintoff	10
S.K. Warne	c Giles b Harmison	2
B. Lee	run out	8
J.W. Gillespie	b S.Jones	13
G.D. McGrath	not out	20
Extras	(B 10, LB 8, NB 8)	26
TOTAL		384

ENGLAND

M.E. Trescothick	c Langer b McGrath	4
A.J. Strauss	c Warne b McGrath	2
*M.P.Vaughan	b McGrath	3
I.R. Bell	b McGrath	6
K.P. Pietersen	c Martyn b Warne	57
A. Flintoff	b McGrath	0
#G.O.Jones	c Gilchrist b Lee	30
A.F. Giles	c Gilchrist b Lee	11
M.J. Hoggard	c Hayden b Warne	0
S.J. Harmison	c Martyn b Lee	11
S.P. Jones	not out	20
Extras	(B 1, LB 5, NB 5)	11
TOTAL		155

M.E. Trescothick	c Hayden b Warne	44
A.J. Strauss	c & b Lee	37
*M.P.Vaughan	b Lee	4
I.R. Bell	lbw b Warne	8
K.P. Pietersen	not out	64
A. Flintoff	c Gilchrist b Warne	3
#G.O.Jones	c Gillespie b McGrath	6
A.F. Giles	c Hayden b McGrath	0
M.J. Hoggard	lbw b McGrath	0
S.J. Harmison	lbw b Warne	0
S.P. Jones	c Warne b McGrath	0
Extras	(B 6, LB 5, NB 3)	14
TOTAL		180

ENGLAND

	O	M	R	W		O	M	R	W
Harmison	11.2	0	43	5		27.4	6	54	3
Hoggard	8	0	40	1		16	1	56	2
Flintoff	11	2	50	2		27	4	123	2
S.Jones	10	0	48	2		18	1	69	1
Giles						11	1	56	0
Bell						1	0	8	0

AUSTRALIA

	O	M	R	W		O	M	R	W
McGrath	18	5	53	5		17.1	2	29	4
Lee	15.1	5	47	3		15	3	58	2
Gillespie	8	1	30	0		6	0	18	0
Warne	7	2	19	2		20	2	64	4

FALL OF WICKETS

Wkt	A 1st	E 1st	A 2nd	E 2nd
1st	35	10	18	80
2nd	55	11	54	96
3rd	66	18	100	104
4th	66	19	255	112
5th	87	21	255	119
6th	126	79	274	158
7th	175	92	279	158
8th	178	101	289	164
9th	178	122	341	167
10th	190	155	384	180

Umpires: Aleem Dar and R.E. Koertzen
TV Umpire: M.R. Benson

Completed match scorecard.

10

Limited Overs Cricket

Limited overs cricket offers results: a definite conclusion within a shortened time span. In so doing it answered one of the major criticisms of the traditional five day Test matches in the 1960s: that games which dragged on for days and then ended in a draw were out of step with the modern world.

While that might have been so – and the limited over game is often aggressive as far as batsmen are concerned – bowling tactics and field settings became negative. A game which was supposed to be attacking instead saw wicket-taking devalued in favour of preventing scoring. Slip fielding began to be dispensed with and fast bowlers and spinners prepared to flight the ball banished for fear of giving away runs.

In the early days there were other casualties too. The limited over batting strategy was based on a steady start so that after 10 overs the score was 0-30, followed by a gradual quickening of the rate so that after 30 overs the total had risen to 2-110., then acceleration by the middle-order strokemakers so that after 40 overs the score was 4-160, and then a wild slog in the last 10 overs would see the total boosted to around 240 runs.

Much has changed and the World Cups which began in 1975 were often the scene for revolutionary tactics. In 1992, for instance, New Zealand used off-spinner Dipak Patel to open the attack and Shane Warne has proved a highly effective bowler in one day international matches. In 1996 Sanath Jayasuriya and Romesh Kaluwitharana rewrote the rules by starting the Sri Lankan innings with explosive strokeplay, a factor which greatly assisted their win that year. To show how the game has changed Australia posted its 100 in the sixteenth over of the 2003 World Cup final at Johannesburg and went on to a record score of 2-359. A most remarkable match occurred at the same ground in 2006 when Australia scored 4-434 from 50 overs and would have been expected to romp away with the match. However, South Africa miraculously overtook the target to reach 9-438 with one ball to spare, the match total of 872 runs surpassing the previous one-day record by 179 runs.

The one day crime is to be dismissed with several overs in hand, but the game has, nevertheless, evolved in a curious way where batsmen are forced to improvise to pierce defensive fields and take run scoring risks which are inappropriate in other forms of cricket. Steering the ball through the vacant gully area scores a lot of runs in one day cricket, but the same stroke has brought about the downfall of many players at Test level when extra fielders are placed in positions to receive catches. The difficulty for many players is being able to adapt from one style of game to the other.

At the same time not all batting has suffered, and some of the most glorious innings by players such as Adam Gilchrist and Ricky Ponting rate well against the giants of yesteryear such as Vivian Richards, David Gower and Dean Jones while Michael Bevan proved himself a master of the endgame. There are some surprises too and turning the clock back twenty-five years English opener Geoff Boycott amazed Australian cricket followers by loosening his customary defensive shackles in giving several outstanding displays in the first World Series Cup matches of the 1979-80 season.

Fielding too has benefited with skills improving dramatically and all players aiming to be athletic and acrobatic. The improvement in cricketers' physical fitness has seen the catching and ground fielding reach spectacular levels and this rise in standards has transferred back into the longer forms of the game.

Perhaps the major benefit, however, relates to over rates. Where the paying public sometimes saw as little as 70 overs per six hour day during the 1980s they were now virtually guaranteed 100 overs in seven hours playing time. It was also a welcome sight to see bowlers bustling into position near the end of an innings to avoid penalties whereas the same men would dawdle throughout the day during a Test match.

The limited over game is impatient as are the people who watch it, and it is the most popular form of cricket now played. Every match has the element of the run chase, and constant mention is made by commentators of comparative run rates throughout an innings. The danger of this game exists in placing too heavy an emphasis on statistics and swamping style completely. The players who reach the top have done so through playing first-class cricket, where the use of a straight bat and bowling aggressively are the necessary ingredients for success. The constant mixing and matching of talents can occasionally take a toll on a player's skills and may be to the detriment of his game as well as to cricket as a whole.

In days gone by first-class cricket was in harmony with the seasons, a sometimes lazy summer game where memory was an important factor in appreciating and judging players' performances. Limited over cricket is about the here and now and few, even great, one-day performances are remembered for very long. The large number of limited over matches contested means that they become blurred for the players who participate in them as well for spectators.

Looking back on the international summer of 2004-05 it is difficult to recall that Hamish Marshall was man of the match in the first game of the inaugural Chappell–Hadlee series or indeed that the rubber was drawn after the third match was abandoned without a ball being bowled. Twenty years ago Australia fought back at the end of a drubbing by the West Indies in Test matches with some exciting performances by opening batsman Kepler Wessells, 19-year-old fast bowler Craig McDermott and 38-year-old leg-spinner Bob Holland whose 10 wicket haul in Sydney brought an innings victory in the last match of the series in Sydney. At the time these performances seemed worth recalling for years but such was the nature of one day selection that Wessells was accused of scoring too slowly, McDermott of being too inexperienced, and Holland not selected at all. The difference over the years has been that the two varieties of the game have been seen as more specialised with players such as Simon O'Donnell and Simon Davis being cast early as limited over exponents and others such as Justin Langer given few opportunities at the one-day level. As time has gone on players like Michael Bevan started in the Test side and became a limited-over specialist while Darren Lehmann moved in a reverse direction.

This swapping or horses-for-courses policy is not always something players take easily as a hero in one form of the game vanishes from another. Mark Taylor's retirement was possibly hastened by his part-time captaincy and Steve Waugh also probably resented his dismissal from the one day leadership and strove (unsuccessfully as it turned out) to win back his position in the Australian team in the short form of the game.

Conditions of Play

Playing conditions for the VB Series of international one-day matches and the ING Cup domestic limited over games are almost the same, except

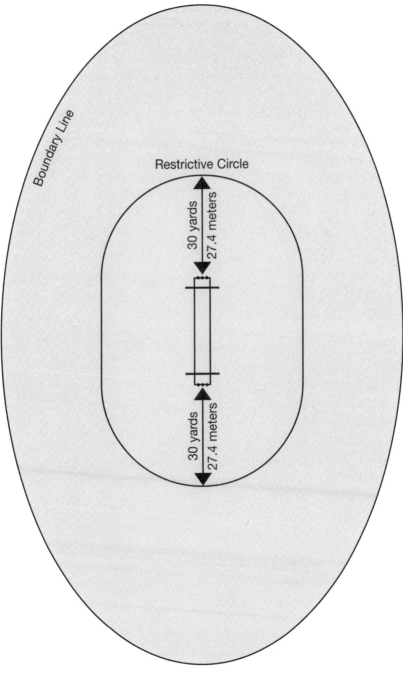

Field Restrictions (limited over games)

for matters relating to the appointment of umpires, penalties for over rates, the format of the finals, and the players code of behaviour and substitutes.

Play is for seven hours, consisting of two three and a half hour sessions separated by an interval of 45 minutes.

In an uninterrupted match the teams normally bat for 50 overs (six balls each) unless dismissed earlier. No bowler is allowed to bowl more than ten overs in an innings.

Field restrictions

A number of restrictions have been applied by Cricket Australia for the conduct of games.

These involve the marking of two semi-circles with a centre at the middle stump at either end of the pitch with a radius of 27.4 metres (30 yards), the ends of each joined by a straight line on the same side of the pitch (see p 73).

For the first 15 overs of each team's innings only two fielders are permitted to be outside this zone when the ball is delivered. The purpose of this rule is to prevent fielding sides adopting excessively negative tactics from the beginning of the match by stacking fielders in the outfield, and it allows batsmen to score freely if they can pick gaps in the field.

From overs 16 to 30 only three fielders are permitted outside the field restriction at the instant of delivery.

For the rest of the innings no more than five fielders may be placed outside the zone, giving both batsmen and fielders flexibility in placing the ball for runs and reducing run-scoring potential.

The limit of the five fielders on the on side throughout an innings sensibly prevents the focus of the bowling attack on that side of the wicket and the curtailing of the handsome off side strokes.

Two inner circles are also drawn on the field, their centres being the centre point of the popping crease at either end of the pitch. The radius of each of these circles is 13.7 metres (15 yards) and the field restriction area should be marked by dots.

In the first 15 overs two stationary fielders must be placed within the 15 yard restriction of the striker although when a fast bowler is operating the fielders may be permitted to stand deeper provided that they are in the slip, leg slip or gully positions.

Interpretation of wides

Umpires are much stricter in their interpretation of *wides* than under the normal Laws of Cricket. This is in order to prevent the deliberate bowling of balls wide of the wicket or over the batsman's head.

Thus a ball passing over head height of the striker's normal stance would be called a wide as would any delivery which *does not give the batsman a reasonable opportunity to score*.

As a guide on the leg side a ball landing clearly outside the leg stump and going further away would be called 'wide' as would a ball passing more than 76.8cm (30 inches) outside the off stump.

No-balls
Underarm bowling was declared illegal in all major cricket following the notorious underarm delivery bowled by Trevor Chappell on the instruction of his brother Greg, the Australian captain, on 1 February 1981. The instruction was given in order to prevent New Zealand scoring six runs off the last ball to tie the third final of the World Series Cup.

In the ING Cup a *free hit* is given after a no-ball for overstepping the popping crease or bowling wide of the return crease. The delivery following such a no-ball shall be the free hit for whichever batsman is facing it. If the delivery for the free hit itself is an illegitimate ball (wide or no-ball) then the next ball will become a free hit.

A bowler is only allowed to bowl one fast short pitched ball per over. When he does so such a ball is advised by the umpire and any further balls will be declared no-balls.

Time wasting, over rate penalties
A number of penalties apply if less than the required number of overs are bowled in the scheduled time. In ING Cup matches if the team fielding fails to bowl its required overs play shall continue until the required number has been bowled. For each over short of the required number 0.5 shall be deducted from the team's match points.

Balls, clothing and screens
White balls are used in Australia's limited over competitions. Sightscreens are black.

The Australian states wear the following colours:

New South Wales	Light Blue and Navy Blue
Victoria	Navy Blue and Light Blue
South Australia	Red and Gold
Queensland	Maroon and Yellow
Western Australia	Gold and Black
Tasmania	Green and Gold

Results

There can only be a result if both teams bat for at least 15 overs, unless one team is dismissed in that time, or the team batting second takes less than that many overs to score the runs necessary for a win. Matches in which one or both teams do not bat 15 overs are declared drawn games.

The team which scores the greater number of runs wins the match irrespective of how many wickets it loses.Thus a side which makes 0-214 would lose to one which made 9-215. In the case of a tie points are divided, the wickets lost are not used for any type of countback.

Complications arise when the team batting second has not had the chance to complete the agreed number of overs.The *Duckworth–Lewis system* accounts for changes in the relative run-scoring resources available to the two teams caused by interruptions. These resources consist of both overs remaining and wickets in hand.

Under Duckworth–Lewis the team batting second will be compensated for losing overs and generally will have their target score adjusted to a smaller total to win the game. If play does not resume the result will depend on the team's score compared with the DL target at the time the match is abandoned.The *par score* shown on scoreboards during the innings of the team batting second is a value determined by the DL method to determine the result of a match if it ended at that moment provided each team had played 25 overs.

History of the One-Day Game

Limited over cricket was introduced in England following a committee report which examined the decline in the traditional game.The Gillette Cup began in England in 1963 and was followed by the John Player League in 1969, and the Benson and Hedges Cup in 1972. In Australia a domestic competition began in 1969-70. Known as the V&G (Vehicle and General) Knockout Cup it was played between the Australian states and New Zealand. It remained with V&G in its second year, and has since been sponsored by Coca-Cola (1971-73), Gillette (1973-79), McDonalds (1979-88), FAI Insurance (1988-92), Mercantile Mutual (1992-2001) and ING (2001-06).

The public appetite thus whetted, needed to be satisfied at the international level. Melbourne, where the first Test match was played, saw the first one-day international match, although it was only programmed to compensate fans for the loss of a Test which was completely abandoned because of rain.

The first game between Australia and England took place on 5 January 1971, and saw Australia win by five wickets. England scored 190 off 39.4 (eight ball) overs and Australia replied with 5-190 from 34.6 overs. John Edrich and Ian Chappell each topped 50 runs but the most remarkable aspect of the game was that nine of the 15 wickets fell to spin bowlers Ashley Mallett, Keith Stackpole and Ray Illingworth. Forty-six thousand people attended the first game but despite its success, limited over internationals had modest beginnings. By 1974 only 15 matches had been held. Three years later, however, the total had ballooned to over 150 matches and the trend has continued.

In Australia the second limited over international match was against England at Melbourne in 1974-75, and one game was played against the West Indies at Adelaide Oval during their 1975-76 tour. Strangely, in the light of its later popularity the Adelaide game was regarded as an unnecessary intervention into the Test series. The heaviest programming of one-day international matches in the early years occurred when four were played as the Benson and Hedges Cup against England during the 1978-79 tour.

The real expansion of one-day cricket came during the split between Kerry Packer's World Series Cricket and the traditional game. The marketing of cricket remained under Packer company PBL Marketing from 1979 until 1994.

Today, limited over games in Australia well outnumber Tests and crowds watch both forms of the game in large numbers. Limited overs cricket is an integral part of the season and has gained in prestige as it has become more sophisticated.

Australian One-Day Internationals

The matches were in Australia known as the Benson and Hedges World Series Cup from 1979 to 1996 after which the competition has been known as the Carlton and United Series (1996-2001) and the VB Series since then. The format of these international games has involved Australia and two other countries playing successive round robin matches in different cities before qualifying for the finals. In 1979-80 Australia, the West Indies and England played eight qualifying matches but the following year the number was raised to ten, twelve (1981-82), ten for the next five years, and back to eight since 1987-88 with the exception of the 1994-95 season. In that summer four sides competed – Australia, Australia A, England and Zimbabwe – with six qualifying matches. However, the experiment was not repeated when England in particular, faced the embarrassment of seeing the Australia A side contest the final ahead of it and Australian captain Mark Taylor objected to cricket followers supporting the underdog A side. The finals were the best of three in 1979-80, best of five in 1980-81 and 1981-82, and best of three since. If two teams tie for second the place in the finals goes to the team with the higher run-rate.

The winners have been as follows:

1979-80	West Indies
1980-81	Australia
1981-82	West Indies
1982-83	Australia
1983-84	West Indies
1984-85	West Indies
1985-86	Australia
1986-87	England
1987-88	Australia
1988-89	West Indies
1989-90	Australia
1990-91	Australia
1991-92	Australia
1992-93	West Indies
1993-94	Australia
1994-95	Australia
1995-96	Australia
1996-97	Pakistan
1997-98	Australia
1998-99	Australia
1999-2000	Australia
2000-01	Australia
2001-02	South Africa
2002-03	Australia
2003-04	Australia
2004-05	Australia
2005-06	Australia

World Cup

Australia's performances in the World Cup have varied. In the very first cup in 1975 international sides were learning how to play the limited over game and Australia did well before going down narrowly to the West Indies in the final. Four years later Australian cricket was still split by

World Series Cricket so that an understrength side led by Kim Hughes failed to make the semi-finals. By 1983 the split had been prepared but the side led again by Hughes underperformed in again not reaching the last four and included the ignominy of being defeated by Zimbabwe in a preliminary match.

The mid-1980s saw Australian Test cricket at a very low ebb but recovery in its cricket fortunes followed its triumph in the fourth cup held in India and Pakistan in 1987.

Australia and New Zealand hosted the trophy in 1992 when the home side again failed to make the finals but it enjoyed a much better campaign in India, Pakistan and Sri Lanka in 1996 before being defeated by Sri Lanka in the final. The last two cups (1999) and (2003) have seen Australia rule although the first in England provided an enormous test of character after losing their second and third qualifying matches to New Zealand and Pakistan and facing the prospect of an early exit. In the last cup in South Africa, Australia was rarely threatened and proved supreme in its final victory.

The winners have been:

1975	West Indies
1979	West Indies
1983	India
1987	Australia
1992	Pakistan
1996	Sri Lanka
1999	Australia
2003	Australia

One-Day Domestic Cricket
Limited over matches among the Australian states began as we have seen in 1969-70 as the V&G Cup Knockout Cup. The original format of the competition was for the six states to play preliminary knockout matches with two then playing in one semi-final and the other playing New Zealand in the other. By taking its place directly in a semi-final New Zealand dominated the first six years of the competition by winning three titles. In 1973-74 New Zealand played six Tests against Australia and star batsman Glenn Turner refused to play in the 1974-75 matches, feeling his country was 'lowering itself' by competing. Turner did appear the following year, however, when New Zealand lost the final to Western Australia. But that was the last time they played in the competition.

From 1976-77 to 1978-79 the program was uneven with two states getting first-round byes each year. When McDonalds took over the sponsorship in 1979-80 the competition was revamped and became fairer. Instead of a knockout the six states were divided into two divisions of three with the leading states from each division each qualifying for the finals.

The Australian Capital Territory competed for three years in the 1990s but the six states have been the mainstays of the competition.

The winners have been:

V&G Knockout Cup

| 1969-70 | New Zealand |
| 1970-71 | Western Australia |

Australasian Knockout Cup

| 1971-72 | Victoria |
| 1972-73 | New Zealand |

Gillette Cup

1973-74	Western Australia
1974-75	New Zealand
1975-76	Queensland
1976-77	Western Australia
1977-78	Western Australia
1978-79	Tasmania

McDonald's Cup

1979-80	Victoria
1980-81	Queensland
1981-82	Queensland
1982-83	Western Australia
1983-84	South Australia
1984-85	New South Wales
1985-86	Western Australia
1986-87	South Australia
1987-88	New South Wales

FAI Insurance Cup

1988-89	Queensland
1989-90	Western Australia
1990-91	Western Australia
1991-92	New South Wales

Mercantile Mutual Cup

| 1992-93 | New South Wales |
| 1993-94 | New South Wales |

1994-95	Victoria
1995-96	Queensland
1996-97	Western Australia
1997-98	Queensland
1998-99	Victoria
1999-2000	Western Australia
2000-01	New South Wales

ING Cup

2001-02	New South Wales
2002-03	New South Wales
2003-04	Western Australia
2004-05	Tasmania
2005-06	New South Wales

11

Pura Cup

The six Australian states compete in the Pura Cup (previously the Sheffield Shield) with each side playing ten matches: five on their home ground and five games away. The two leading states then contest a final, the choice of venue being the home ground of the state which finishes in top position.

Pura Cup games last for four days with six hours play scheduled per day. The minimum number of overs to be bowled is 96 less breaks for interruptions such as wickets falling, injuries, bad light and rain. On the last day a minimum of 80 overs must be bowled other than the last hour of the match when again 16 overs must be bowled with one exception. If, after 30 minutes of the last hour has elapsed both captains accept that there is no prospect of a result they may agree to cease play.

Results of Pura Cup matches are determined by the following points system of scoring:

For an outright win after leading on the first innings	6
For an outright win after a tie on the first innings	6
For an outright win after being behind on the first innings	6
For a tie where both teams have completed two innings	3
For a first innings lead even if beaten outright	2
For an outright loss after leading on the first innings	2
For a tie on the first innings and no outright result	1
For an outright loss after a tie on the first innings	1
For a loss on the first innings	0
Abandoned or drawn matches with no first innings result	0

The Sheffield Shield began as a result of a donation of £150 by the Earl of Sheffield, the manager of the English touring team to Australia in 1891-92. The Earl made the donation to further Australian cricket and the following year the Australasian Cricket Council started the competition with three colonies – New South Wales, Victoria and South Australia – competing.

In the early years these colonies and then states played each other twice and Queensland did not enter the competition until 1926-27 because of the high costs of sending teams north by rail. In that year South Australia won the Shield on percentage as it played only five games against six by the other states, and did not play Queensland in Brisbane.

Western Australia did not enter the Shield until 1947-48 and surprisingly won in its first season, although it played a restrictive program, contesting only four matches to the other states' seven. It first played full-time in 1956-57 and its first Sheffield Shield victory on an even footing was in the 1967-68 season. Tasmania was admitted to the Sheffield Shield on a restricted basis in 1977-78 and gained full membership in 1982-83.

Not surprisingly the most populous states, New South Wales (44) and Victoria (26) have had the greatest success, although Western Australia (14) proved dominant in the 1970s and 1980s, and South Australia's 13 wins have come at regular intervals. Queensland's search for a win became something of a search for cricket's Holy Grail but after their initial success in 1994-95 they have a stronger winning habit with five further titles.

Interstate cricket is the final grooming ground for Australia's Test players but the Shield's spectator appeal fell dramatically in response to the assault of the limited over game. With losses on the competition amounting to around $6 million a year it was probably not surprising that the Australian Cricket Board sold the event to National Foods Limited and renamed it the Pura Milk Cup. While traditionalists were shocked – the 'Milk' lasted only one year – it has to be said that Lord Sheffield's naming rights had proved a bargain over 108 years. One state which certainly didn't mind the changed of name was Tasmania. As they wryly observed the new competition began with all states equal.

Sheffield Shield

1892-93	Victoria		1899-1900	New South Wales
1893-94	South Australia		1900-01	Victoria
1894-95	Victoria		1901-02	New South Wales
1895-96	New South Wales		1902-03	New South Wales
1896-97	New South Wales		1903-04	New South Wales
1897-98	Victoria		1904-05	New South Wales
			1905-06	New South Wales

1898-99	Victoria		1953-54	New South Wales
1906-07	New South Wales		1954-55	New South Wales
1907-08	Victoria		1955-56	New South Wales
1908-09	New South Wales		1956-57	New South Wales
1909-10	South Australia		1957-58	New South Wales
1910-11	New South Wales		1958-59	New South Wales
1911-12	New South Wales		1959-60	New South Wales
1912-13	South Australia		1960-61	New South Wales
1913-14	New South Wales		1961-62	New South Wales
1914-15	Victoria		1962-63	Victoria
1915-19	Matches suspended		1963-64	South Australia
1919-20	New South Wales		1964-65	New South Wales
1920-21	New South Wales		1965-66	New South Wales
1921-22	Victoria		1966-67	Victoria
1922-23	New South Wales		1967-68	Western Australia
1923-24	Victoria		1968-69	South Australia
1924-25	Victoria		1969-70	Victoria
1925-26	New South Wales		1970-71	South Australia
1926-27	South Australia		1971-72	Western Australia
1927-28	Victoria		1972-73	Western Australia
1928-29	New South Wales		1973-74	Victoria
1929-30	Victoria		1974-75	Western Australia
1930-31	Victoria		1975-76	South Australia
1931-32	New South Wales		1976-77	Western Australia
1932-33	New South Wales		1977-78	Western Australia
1933-34	Victoria		1978-79	Victoria
1934-35	Victoria		1979-80	Victoria
1935-36	South Australia		1980-81	Western Australia
1936-37	Victoria		1981-82	South Australia
1937-38	New South Wales		1982-83	New South Wales
1938-39	South Australia		1983-84	Western Australia
1939-40	New South Wales		1984-85	New South Wales
1940-46	Matches suspended		1985-86	New South Wales
1946-47	Victoria		1986-87	Western Australia
1947-48	Western Australia		1987-88	Western Australia
1948-49	New South Wales		1988-89	Western Australia
1949-50	New South Wales		1989-90	New South Wales
1950-51	Victoria		1990-91	Victoria
1951-52	New South Wales		1991-92	Western Australia
1952-53	South Australia		1992-93	New South Wales

1993-94	New South Wales
1994-95	Queensland
1995-96	South Australia
1996-97	Queensland
1997-98	Western Australia
1998-99	Western Australia

Pura Milk Cup

1999-2000	Queensland

Pura Cup

2000-01	Queensland
2001-02	Queensland
2002-03	New South Wales
2003-04	Victoria
2004-05	New South Wales
2005-06	Queensland

12

It's Not Cricket

The expression 'it's not cricket' is used to suggest some connotation of foul play. In 2004 Australian wicket-keeper Adam Gilchrist controversially revived an old practice of batsmen walking from the crease when they were out. At one time this practice was claimed as the special reserve of Englishmen (walkers) while Australians were not. Traditionally Australians preferred to let the umpires make the decision. Confusion has certainly been caused when players believed to be walkers have awaited the umpire's decision at the wicket. If such players were then given out some doubt was placed in the public's mind because of the cricketer's perceived fairness and the umpire was often assumed (wrongly) to have given an incorrect decision.

Since the 1970s, however, cricket has generally had little time for sentiment. Bowlers and fielders are aggressive with their appeals and their accompanying antics are aimed at pressuring the umpires. Often there is no edge of bat on ball in a catch to slip, or there is a definite nick onto the pad in an appeal for lbw. Since the fielding sides work on the premise that sooner or later the umpire will make a mistake – and that will be to their advantage – batsman are less likely to give their wickets away, but may indulge in a little gamesmanship of their own.

One ruse which has been common for a long time is the quick movement by the batsman out of the line of the stumps when an lbw appeal is made. Indeed, batsmen are frequently eager to take off for a run in such circumstances, or at least pretend to do so. Certainly the umpire has little time to make the most difficult of all decisions, and as he can often be in doubt, the benefit goes to the batsman. These actions, while not within the best spirit of the game, do not contravene its laws but have led to a preamble, 'The Spirit of Cricket', being inserted into the Laws of the game in 2000.

Spirit of Cricket

In the preamble it is argued that part of cricket's 'unique appeal' is the good spirit in which it is played but such self-congratulation ignores the fact that golf is a far more moral game given that players are often required to call penalties against themselves. At the elite level golf is also a far better mannered game.

Playing cricket in the proper spirit involves respecting one's opponents, one's captain and team, the umpires, and the game's perceived traditions. It is against the spirit of the game to dispute umpires' decisions, to abuse either opponents or umpires, or to cheat or be involved in sharp practice.

In effect there seems little need for the preamble because it merely summarises some of the laws. However, it throws the onus of responsibility of a team's behaviour on the team captain and calls on umpires to take action against players showing dissent or bringing the game into disrepute.

The laws govern fair and unfair play (as will be explained) and umpires are authorised to intervene in cases of time wasting, damaging the pitch, dangerous bowling and ball tampering.

Unfair Play

Law 42 governs fair and unfair play. For example the *condition of the ball may not be changed*. Any member of the fielding side may polish the ball as long as such polishing does not waste time, and artificial substances such as hair creams are not used. Post-war Australian fast bowler Keith Miller's action of running his hands through his brylcreemed hair and then applying grease to the ball brought complaints fifty years ago while England pace bowler John Lever was accused of rubbing the ball on a sweatband around his head during a tour of India in the 1970s, so the problem is not new.

The ball may not be rubbed on the ground either, nor may its seam be lifted. On the 1970-71 tour of Australia English fast bowler John Snow frequently picked at the ball with his thumbnail and then ironically complained that it was out of shape. However, the most recent accusation of *ball tampering* in Australia was directed at the visiting Pakistani team in their opening tour match against Western Australia in 1995-96. The Australian Cricket Board impounded the ball after umpires Terry Prue and Ross Emerson revealed concern about scarring to one side of the ball although the matter was not raised again.

A second example of unfair play involves *annoying or distracting the striker* while he is receiving the ball and *sledging* is a term for verbal abuse aimed at upsetting the batsman. In the last thirty years there have been numerous examples of fiery exchanges with some of the game's leading players being among the most notable offenders. While Ian Chappell's early 1970s teams were given the moniker 'Ugly Australians' (for their moustaches and bad dress sense as much as their toughness) the superb teams led by Mark Taylor and Steve Waugh in more recent times have occasionally blotted their copybooks by playing too hard.

One of the biggest problems in the game in the 1970s was *intimidatory* bowling, which forced the appearance of protective headgear. Fast bowlers readily admit that they bowl a bouncer to unsettle the batsman and the bouncer is a legitimate shock weapon. The matter is left in the hands of the umpires but deliberate short-pitched bowling aimed with the intention of hitting the batsman has shell-shocked a succession of fine players. A *short-pitched ball* is not clearly defined in the law but it includes a ball passing above head height to a batsman standing upright at the crease.

The umpires are advised to adopt the following procedures for dealing with the offence if they consider such bowling unfair. In the first place the bowler's end umpire should call and signal 'no-ball' and inform his co-umpire, the captain and the batsmen. If this action is ineffective the bowler's end umpire should repeat the above procedure and indicate to the bowler that this is his final warning. Should the bowler ignore such a warning the bowler's end umpire should call and signal 'no-ball' and direct that the bowler be removed from the attack for the remainder of the innings. He should then report the occurrence to the umpire, the batsmen, the captain of the batting side, the management of the fielding side and the governing body controlling the match who may then decide to take further action action against the fielding captain and the bowler concerned.

A second type of intimidatory bowling is the bowling of fast high full tosses or *beam balls* at the batsmen. Such an action brings the same cautions and warnings as for short-pitched bowling. The high full pitch is one which is above waist height of the striker when standing upright at the crease. A recent case which created a great deal of ire was Brett Lee's beam ball which struck New Zealand wicket-keeper Brendon McCullum on the hand in a one-day international match at Auckland in 2005, and which saw some reporters calling for Lee to be sent home from the Australian's tour.

Time wasting was the bane of the game in the 1980s and particularly in Test matches. On the third day of the Third Test between Australia and the West Indies at Adelaide in 1984-85 the West Indies bowlers sent down only 69 overs (414 balls) in a day's play. On the same ground on the last day of the Fourth Test between the same two countries in 1960-61 the West Indies bowled 113.1 eight ball overs (905 balls) in an attempt to win the match. The attack was, of course, different: in 1984-85 the bowlers were all fast whereas in the earlier game they consisted of the world's fastest bowler (Wesley Hall), one medium-pacer (Frank Worrell), one fast medium and spin (Gary Sobers), and two spinners (Lance Gibbs and Alf Valentine). Even so, the difference in the amount of actual play was staggering.

The slowing down of play by the fielding side is often said to have begun under Len Hutton's captaincy on the 1954-55 English tour of Australia and the attritional tactic was adopted by captains to prevent batsmen having too many balls to hit. To the list of Ways of Being Dismissed which appeared in Chapter 2 perhaps should be added *frustrated out*: a batsman not merely wanting the *right* ball to hit but *a* ball, and instead getting out to a wild stroke.

Bowlers are, of course, not the only people to blame. Batsmen too waste time checking field settings, patting down patches of turf on the pitch, and holding conversations with their partners. All these acts are objects of speculation for commentators but hardly riveting action for spectators. In the past these devices, plus the inevitable adjustment of pads and tying of shoelaces were carried out most conspicuously just before an interval or close of play. The one advantage of an International Cricket Council regulation of 1993 requiring that a minimum of 90 overs be bowled in a day in a Test match has been the elimination of such actions due to play generally ending when the overs are completed.

The umpires may caution, warn, and report both sides for time wasting, and award five penalty runs to the opposing sides, but the real solutions remain with the game's administrators. Players are forced to play extra time to bowl the required number of overs but this, in itself, is not an ideal solution. If it is good enough for the law to stipulate that a batsman should always be ready to take strike when a bowler is ready to start his run up the opposite should also apply. Test cricketers are sporting professionals who are paid well. There is no reason why spectators should be forced into overtime by watching play for seven hours which ought to be completed in six.

Damaging the pitch is an example of unfair play which is strictly policed by the umpires. In most cases bowlers infringe by running too close to the stumps and then continuing down the pitch in their follow-through.

The bowler is then cautioned by the umpire at his end, warned, and if he continues to offend is penalised by being removed from the attack for the rest of the innings. Even when no infringement has occurred commentators frequently mention spin bowlers pitching the ball into the 'bowler's footmarks'. These marks are those which have been legitimately left on the pitch in a bowler's follow-through, but may nevertheless assist another bowler without being unfair.

A *protected area* on the pitch is defined as that area contained by an imaginary line parallel to the popping creases and 1.52 metres (5 feet) in front of them, and within two imaginary lines drawn from points on that line to the two middle stumps and 30.48 centimetres (1 foot) either side of the middle stumps.

There are other examples of unfair play that are not covered in the laws which can prove a dilemma for umpires. For example, there may be a situation in which the batsmen start for a run and the fielder attempts to get the ball and run one of them out. However, the batsman then deliberately places himself in a direct line between the thrower and the wicket, and is prepared to be hit in the back to avoid being run out. In this example the batsman is taking an unfair advantage and if he was knocked down by the throw the umpire could immediately call 'dead ball' in which case a run out would not be allowed. On the other hand if he let the play take its course the batsman who was stunned mid-pitch could be dismissed. It would be an awkward dismissal.

Other incidents sometimes see batsmen trying to make a run when the ball is in the vicinity of the bowler's wicket, and as a result a collision with a fielder or bowler may result. While a bowler or fielder may have as many rights as the batsman to occupy an area near the pitch in trying to effect a run out their play can be unfair if they obstruct the batsman. Something like this occurred in the notorious Lillee–Miandad incident which took place on 16 November 1981 during the First Test between Australia and Pakistan in Perth.

Dennis Lillee, who was bowling, stood on the pitch and partially confronted Javed Miandad, who brushed him as he ran past to complete his run. Lillee then kicked Miandad, who reacted angrily by raising his bat as if to strike Lillee. As a result Lillee was suspended for two one-day international matches. It followed a series of controversies and caused conditions relating to players conduct being framed in the Laws of Cricket in 1980 and led eventually to the Australian Cricket Board and its successor Cricket Australia implementing a Code of Behaviour to be observed by players. Over the years the code has become more and more detailed and the current code exhaustively spells out offences and penalties.

Cricket Australia Code of Behaviour

There are four levels of offences.

At level 1 there are such things as the abuse of cricket equipment or clothing, ground equipment, fixtures and fittings; showing dissent at an umpire's decision; using language that is obscene, offensive or insulting, or making obscene gestures; engaging in excessive appealing; aggressively pointing or gesturing towards the pavilion to a batsman who has been dismissed. While considered relatively minor they include batsmen knocking or kicking their stumps down, bashing their bats on the fence or smashing dressing room windows.

Level 2 offences include showing serious dissent at an umpire's decision; deliberate physical contact with another player or umpire; charging or advancing towards an umpire when appealing; deliberately and maliciously distracting or obstructing a player or umpire on the field; throwing the ball at or near a player or umpire in a dangerous way; using language that is obscene, offensive or insulting to another player, official or spectator; changing the condition of the ball and so on. Serious dissent at an umpire's decision may include such actions (by a bowler) as shaking the head, snatching the cap, pointing at a pad or inside edge of the bat or (by a batsman) of excessive delay in leaving the wicket when dismissed.

Level 3 offences may be such things as intimidating an umpire or referee; threatening assault on other players, team officials or spectators; and using language or gestures which 'offend, insult, humiliate, intimidate, threaten, disparage, or vilify another person on the basis of that person's race, religion, colour, descent or national or ethnic origin'.

Level 4 offences involve threats of assault against umpires or officials; actual assaults on players, umpires, officials or spectators; other acts of on-field violence; and using language or gestures that seriously offend, insult, humiliate persons as outlined above.

Apart from the four levels players and officials must not engage in behaviour which is regarded as 'unbecoming' or likely to bring the game into disrepute. Players must obey Cricket Australia's Anti-Doping Policy and those such as Shane Warne who offended against the policy just prior to the World Cup in 2003 were suspended in accordance with that policy.

Players and officials must not engage in betting or gambling on matches; induce or encourage others to bet on matches; attempt to contrive the result of a match; fail to attempt to play to the best of one's ability; take a reward for information about the weather, the state of the ground, team composition, players form and tactics; or engage in other corrupt conduct which might affect the result of a game or event.

Players and officials must not make public comments in which they denigrate other players or officials; a country in which they are touring; the home country of a visiting team; or comment or criticise likely outcomes of hearings, reports and appeals.

Finally, players and officials must obey Cricket Australia's Racial and Religious Vilification Code and Anti-Harassment Policy.

Penalties depend on the nature of the offences, the harm caused, the standing of the player or official, the degree of remorse shown, and the prior record of the offender. They can include reprimands, bans, fines, directing that offenders make reparation for damage caused, and requiring that offenders undergo counselling. Maximum penalties may include life bans for severe offences such as assault.

13

Glossary

Across the flight
Playing with an oblique or cross bat.

Agricultural shot
Colourful phrase popularised by the commentator Frank Tyson which suggests that the striker might be as adept with a scythe as a bat.

All-rounder
Players who excels in more than one department of the game.

Along the line
Playing with a straight bat.

Analysis(es)
Individual performances of members of a bowling attack expressed in terms of overs bowled, runs scored from those overs, and wickets taken.

Angle the bat
A batting technique whereby the batsman keeps his wrists well ahead of the blade so that the ball is directed safely to the ground.

Appeal
A call or cry of 'How's that?' (more often, 'Howzat?') by one or more members of the fielding side when they believe (or want the umpire to believe) a batsman is out. Usually the appeal is directed to one umpire only, but sometimes the other is asked to adjudicate or affirm a decision. In many instances – such as being bowled or obviously caught – no appeal is made and the batsman walks from the wicket promptly. But in cases of lbw, low catches, stumping and run out decisions, where millimetres may decide a batsman's fate, he will await the umpire's ruling.

Arm ball
A ball delivered by an orthodox spinner (right-arm off-spinner of left-arm leg-spinner) which goes on with his arm rather than taking it's

Dicko 2005

APPEAL

normal turn. Frequently used with change of pace in an attempt to bowl a batsman or have him caught at the wicket.

Ashes

Mythical trophy which remains at Lord's but is the stake in Test series between Australia and England. Dates from a notice which appeared as a mock obituary in the *Sporting Times* the day after England was defeated by Australia for the first time in England in 1882. It read:

> In Affectionate Remembrance
> of
> ENGLISH CRICKET
> which died at The Oval
> on
> 29th August 1882.
> Deeply Lamented by a large circle of
> Sorrowing Friends and Acquaintances
> RIP
> The body will be cremated
> and the Ashes taken to Australia.

The Ashes have a spiritual rather than an actual significance.

Attack

A complement of bowlers and their action as a unit in a given match.

Attacking cricket

A style of play most favoured by cricket watchers, where batsmen aim to score runs at a quick rate against bowlers who are trying to take their wickets, and fielders who are placed in catching rather than run-saving positions.

Back foot strokes

Strokes played against short-pitched balls with the weight transferred onto the rear leg.

Backing up

(1) The action of the non-striking batsman advancing a metre or two down the pitch in order to gain an advantage when making quick runs. See **Mankad**.

(2) The action of a fielder running behind a fellow fielder in order to act as a second line of defence; or in moving behind a wicket-keeper of fielder taking the ball at the stumps, so as to prevent overthrows when batsmen are running.

Bails

The two bails are each 10.95 cm (4.32 inches) long and sit in grooves atop the stumps. They must not project more than 1.27cm (0.5 inch) above them.

Ball

(1) A key instrument in play, usually made of leather.

(2) Single delivery bowled.

Ball!

See **Top Cod.**

Bat

(1) Instrument with which the wicket is defended, usually made of English willow.

Bat-pad

A ball which strikes the bat first and then the pad. Close leg-side fielders are often strategically positioned to catch balls which deflect in such a manner and offer a catch.

Bats/Batters

Americanism for the specialist batsmen. Expression widely used in women's cricket.

Batting order

Usually a consistent feature of a side with specialist batsmen succeeded by all-rounders, wicket-keepers and specialist bowlers, and often referred to as top order, middle order and tail-enders.

Beam ball

A fast full toss aimed at the chest and above intentionally or unintentionally. The most dangerous delivery in the game.

Beaten by/in flight

A description of a batsman who makes a false stroke or mistimes the ball because because he has been deceived by its flight.

Beaten for pace

A description of a batsman, who in attempting to play a stroke, misses the ball because of the sheer speed of the delivery.

Blind spot

A weakness in every batsman which a bowler, in finding a perfect length ball, exploits by catching him in two minds whether to play back of forward, and so brings about his dismissal.

Blind swipe

A stroke which could go anywhere but is aggressive in its intent.

Blob

Less familiar colloquialism for failing to score (see also Duck).

Block

(1) The spot where a batsman may choose to rest his bat and which is signified to him by an umpire at the start of his innings.

(2) A defensive stroke which stops the ball which thereby runs only a minimal distance.

Block hole

A small depression dug by a batsman behind the popping crease when he has taken block or guard from the umpire.

Bodyline

Method of intimidatory bowling employed by English captain Douglas Jardine and fast bowlers Harold Larwood and Bill Voce in 1932-33, with the primary aim of restricting the scoring abilities of Don Bradman. Bodyline was offensive bowling in which the attack was directed at chest height and sustained on the line of the leg stump (or batsman's body) with a close ring of fielders awaiting the defensive prods of batsmen trying to protect their hearts and ribs.

Bosey

See **Googly, Wrong'un**. Named after its inventor, B.J.T. Bosanquet and used most often in England.

Bouncer

See Bumper. A fast, short-pitched ball intended to unsettle the nerve of the batsman.

Boundary

(1) The limit of the playing arena of a cricket ground which may be designated by a fence, a rope, or a set of flags, within the circumference of the arena.

(2) A stroke which reaches the boundary and is awarded four runs or is hit over it and awarded six runs.

Box

Protective device for the genitals, usually made of metal or plastic, and either worn inside a jock strap or strapped from the waist.

Break

An alternative term for spin of which there are two varieties: off and leg-spin.

Break-back

Unfamiliar, if not antiquated, expression for an off-break delivered at medium pace.

Building an innings

Action of a batsman who may omit risky strokes from his repertoire, or concentrate on defence in the early stages of his innings before taking command of the bowling.

Bump ball

An expression for a ball which is struck into the ground but at such a precise moment that when it flies up and is caught it gives the impression to spectators of being a legitimate catch. Joking fielders sometimes prey on their audience by throwing the ball into the air to simulate a real catch.

Bumper

See **Bouncer**.

Bunny

See **Rabbit**.

Buying a wicket

(1) Action of a bowler who is willing to give away a few runs while laying a plan to deceive a batsman by change of flight or pace.

(2) Action of a captain willing to risk an unorthodox, if expensive, bowler in the hope of breaking a threatening partnership.

Bye

When a ball, which is neither a wide or a no-ball, passes the striker without touching him or his bat any runs obtained are entered as byes. This is usually caused by a blemish on the part of the wicket-keeper, but frequently (as on the final ball of an innings in one-day games) the batsmen will attempt to run a bye to a wicket-keeper standing back.

Call

Batsmen running together usually operate by a system of calls 'yes', 'no' and 'wait'. The striker usually calls for runs for shots played in front of the wicket and the non-striker for those made behind the wicket. For second and subsequent runs, however, the call should be made by the batsman running to the end nearest the player who is fielding the ball.

Came into him

A ball which moves into a batsman from the off side either from the air or off the pitch.

Carrying one's bat

When a player goes in first and remains not out at the end of his team's innings.

Change bowler

A bowler who is brought into the attack to spell the regular bowlers. Such bowlers often capture wickets when the batsmen relax concentration.

Change of innings

A break of ten minutes is allowed in first-class matches between one team being dismissed or declaring its innings closed and the other taking its place at the wicket. In one-day matches a lunch interval is usually taken at this time.

Cherry

A colloquial term for a new ball which is bright red in appearance.

Chinaman

Although a matter of dispute, an off-break bowled by a left-arm bowler.

Chuck

See **Throw, No-ball**

Clean bowled

When a ball beats the batsman and hits the stumps without having first made contact with the bat, or part of the body of the striker.

Close of play

The end of play for the day, usually a prescribed time, but sometimes delayed in order to ensure that a certain number of overs are bowled in a day's play, and sometimes advanced on account of stoppages for rain and bad light. See **Stumps**.

Close the innings

See **Declaration**.

Cod

See **Ball!**, **Top Cod**.

Collar the bowling

Expression used to describe a situation when a batsman is in complete control of the bowling and is scoring at a rapid rate. Other variants are having the attack by the scruff of the neck or at the batsman's mercy.

Covers

(1) Off side fielding positions

(2) Tarpaulins used for covering the pitch and outfield.

Covering up

The action by a batsman of moving in front of his stumps in order to defend his wicket with his bat or pads.

Cow corner

Area from where a cow shot is expected to be retrieved.

Cow shot

A swipe from outside off stump to the direction of mid-wicket. Possibly derived from a 'cow of a shot'.

Cross bat

Strokes which quite properly employ a horizontal bat are the cuts, pulls, hooks and sweeps. Drives and defensive strokes should be played with a straight bat.

COLLAR
THE BOWLING

Dance down the wicket
  See **Getting to the pitch of the ball**.

Declaration
  A captain may declare his innings closed before all members of his team have batted. This frequently occurs when a side has scored heavily and the captains wants to ensure that he has enough time to bowl his opponents out in order to secure victory. A declaration may be made in either innings, but features more often in the second when a side has established a good first innings lead over its rival, and then scores quickly to build its advantage. Enterprising captains can use declarations to put life into dull games, particularly those which have been considerably reduced by rain interruptions.

Dead ball
  When a ball is 'dead' meaningful play is suspended because a wicket cannot be taken nor can runs be scored. Dead balls are signalled on occasions as outlined in Chapter 8, but also at other times such as:

  (1) when the ball has settled in the hands of a wicket-keeper or bowler
  (2) when it has reached or passed over a boundary
  (3) when over or time is called
  (4) if it lodges in the dress of the batsman or the umpire
  (5) when a batsman is out
  (6) if the batsman on strike is not ready to receive a ball
  (7) if a bowler drops a ball prior to delivery

Dead bat
  Describes a defensive stroke in which a skilful player is able to loosen his grip on the bat so that when he makes contact with the ball it drops at his feet, thus minimising his chances of being caught. See **Soft hands**.

Delivery
  A ball put in motion through the action of bowling.

Departure
  The trek between the batting crease and the dressing-room door after being dismissed. Feelings vary between misery and glory.

Dig
  A colloquial expression for innings. **Second dig** is a second innings.

Dig in
  A batsman who is playing himself in.

Dig out
  (1) A stroke where a batsman has to use all of his resourcefulness to

prevent himself being bowled. Often describes the late jamming down of the bat on a yorker.

(2) A secondary meaning applies to a bowler whose task it is to dig out or remove a batsman.

Dismissal

To get the batsman out. There are 10 ways of being dismissed. For further details see Chapter 2.

Doing a bit

A ball who is making the ball swing through the air, or cutting or spinning it off the pitch.

Doosra

A leg break bowled with an off-break action. Used by off-spinners such as Saqlain Mushtaq and Muttiah Murilatharan.

Draw

A match with an indefinite ending. Usually a Test match because other first-class games such as Pura Cup games, and first grade games give rewards to higher first innings scores.

Drift

A ball which swerves through the air at a slow space.

Drinks

Interval in play, usually midway through a session in first-class games, and in limited over games at the discretion of the captain. In oppressively hot weather more breaks for drinks are sometimes taken.

Drive back onto wicket

An action instigated by a bowler through change of pace or flight which forces a batsman back to defend his stumps, and raises the possibility of dismissing him bowled or hit wicket.

Duck

Being dismissed without scoring. In major Australian international matches since the 1980s a forlorn Daffy Duck has proven a popular TV invention and follows departing batsmen to the dressing-room.

Edge

Batting stroke made with the edge of the bat and likely to bring about the striker's dismissal to a catch behind the wicket. There are several types: inside edge, outside edge, top edge, bottom edge, thick edge, and a thin (or fine) edge.

Entrenched

A batsman who has dug himself in.

Express

A very fast ball or bowler.

Extras

Runs scored but not by the batsman. Consist of byes, leg byes, no-balls, wides and some penalty runs. Batsmen may score from no-balls and receive credit for so doing. See also **Sundries**.

Farming

(1) A good batsman often manages to sustain a long partnership with a lower order batsman by 'farming the strike' or keeping the strike to himself.

(2) Less common term for **Gardening**.

Feel

This term has two diverse meanings:

(1) To feel for the ball when batting is to betray uncertainty and tentativeness.

(2) It can also mean surety and control, particularly regarding timing and assessing the pace of the wicket.

Ferret

A batsman with even less ability than a **Rabbit** and thus goes in after them.

Field

(1) The playing arena.

(2) The arrangement of players on the arena who are supporting the bowler in his efforts to dismiss the batsman.

First-class cricket

A first-class cricket match must be designated as such by the cricketing authority of a country; involve a substantial number of first-class players; and last for three days. In Australia, Test matches, Pura Cup games and contests between touring national sides and the states have such status. The Rest of the World tour played under the auspices of the Australian Cricket Board in 1971-72 was considered first-class but World Series Supertests arranged by Kerry Packer's World Series Cricket in 1977-78 and 1978-79 were not. International and domestic limited over games, while involving first-class players, are not first-class matches.

Flash

A high-speed swish of the bat generally outside the off stump which never connects the ball.

Flashy player

One who looks good but signifies nothing.

Flat track

An even pitch which favours the batsman.

Flat track bully

Batsman who destroys bowling attacks in conditions which favour him. A charge chiefly levelled at Zimbabwean-Englishman Graham Hick and at Matthew Hayden in the early part of his career.

Flight

A technique of varying the trajectory of the ball in order to deceive the batsman. An important weapon for spin bowlers.

Flipper

A variety of the top-spinner and googly, an an extension of the repertoire of right-arm leg-spin bowlers. Invented by Clarrie Grimmett in the 1930s and passed on to Richie Benaud twenty years later. It was rarely seen in the 1970s and 1980s due to the absence of wrist spinners but its best exponent in modern times has been Shane Warne in the first part of his career before shoulder problems intervened. The ball is held in the tips of the first and third fingers and flipped out of the hand from beneath the wrist.

Fly slip

An unorthodox fielding position situated between slips and third man.

Follow-on

Batting sides which fall 200 or more runs behind their opponents first innings score in Test matches may be 'asked' or 'invited' to bat again but, in fact, have no option but to do so. The captain doing the asking does not forfeit his second innings but reserves it until later if necessary.

Forcing strokes

The more powerful strokes, particularly the drives.

Foxing

Tactics employed by the game's tricksters.

(1) Batsmen sometimes pretend they are having difficulty with a bowler by deliberately missing the ball or edging it in order to fool the fielding captain into keeping that bowler operating.

(2) Bowlers may request a field change such as the placement of the fielder on the deep square leg boundary. The batsmen then may anticipate a short ball to hook but receives a succession of balls which are well pitched up.

(3) Fielders try to confuse batsmen by running alongside the ball in order that they risk an extra run when to do so would endanger them and cause a run out.

Front foot strokes
Strokes made from the front foot against deliveries which are pitched well up.

Full pitch
See **Full toss**.

Full toss
(1) A ball which reaches the batsman on the full and is usually easily disposed of by the batsman driving or placing it through the field.
(2) By contrast, often an effective delivery at the end of one-day games because although easily driven it can often be cut off by deep fielders and is difficult to hit over the boundary.

Gardening
The action of a batsman who repairs the pitch by prodding or patting down pieces of turf between deliveries. Often a nervous habit rather than a functional exercise.

Gate
A gap between bat and pad through which batsmen are frequently bowled.

Getting rid of
A colloquial term for dismissing a batsman.

Getting to the pitch of the ball
Enterprising batsmen use their feet against slow bowlers by leaving the crease so as to hit the ball and smother the spin. Of present Australian batsmen Michael Clarke is particularly fast on his feet.

Glide
An alternative term for the leg glance but also used to describe a stroke where the batsman opens the face of the bat and places the ball between slips and gully on the off side.

Goes away
A ball which leaves the batsman in flight or off the pitch.

Gone
(1) Usually associated with the cry 'he's gone' from a commentator meaning the batsman is out.
(2) A secondary meaning relates to a batsman having lost his confidence or nerve to such an extent that his dismissal is imminent.

Good length
A delivery which causes uncertainty in the mind of the batsman so that he does not know whether to play back or forward. A major attribute of bowling.

Googly

See also **Bosey, Wrong'un**. A ball which spins from the off although delivered with an action which resembles a leg break but with the back of the wrist facing the batsman. A skilful disguise in the hands of top exponents such as Mushtaq Ahmed and Stuart MacGill.

Grubber

A delivery which shoots and runs along the ground. A devastating ball in the days of underarm cricket.

Guard

See **Block**. In Australia batsmen usually ask for middle or leg stump in taking their stance at the wicket before receiving their first ball.

Half tracker

Ball pitched half way down the wicket. See **Long hop**.

Half volley

A ball which strikes the bat just after hitting the ground.

Hat trick

A performance whereby a bowler captures three wickets with consecutive balls. The feat usually occurs in one over, but may be spread over two overs, and in some instances over two innings of the same match, but not different matches.

Held the ball back

A deception on the part of the bowler, releasing the ball at a slower pace than a normal delivery.

Hit against the spin

A risky stroke often played with the intention of seizing the initiative from bowlers who are attacking the batsman with a majority of fielders on one side of the wicket.

Hit over the top

An aggressive tactic in which a batsman lofts the ball over the infield which is positioned to restrict run scoring opportunities.

Hoick

See **Agricultural stroke**.

Iffy stroke

A shot which is generally unsound in the method of its execution and likely to bring about a batsman's dismissal. Also described as an injudicious or rash stroke.

In

This term refers to the two batsmen (striker and non-striker) who are at the wicket, and to the batting side as a whole.

Infield

The close and medium-range fielders.

In full flight/stride

A batsman who is playing with ease and scoring rapidly.

Inners

A pair of soft gloves worn by wicket-keepers inside their normal gloves.

Innings

(1) For an individual batsman an innings relates to his play from the time he receives his first ball until he is dismissed, or in the case of not out innings until the rest of his team is dismissed, a declaration is made, or time elapses.

(2) Team innings may be abbreviated but when allowed to run full course consist of ten batsmen each playing an innings before being dismissed, and an eleventh batsman remaining not out.

(3) In first-class matches teams usually have two innings each but one-day limited over matches are single innings affairs.

In the middle

(1) Play in progress in the centre of the ground.

(2) A batsman who is timing the ball well and hitting the ball in the middle of his bat.

Intimidation

Threatening action usually by bowlers and fielders against batsmen but occasionally the reverse when players like Vivian Richards, Ian Botham or Adam Gilchrist have been in full flight.

Intimidatory bowling

The persistent tactic of fast bowlers pitching the ball short to batsmen may constitute intimidation, and an umpire may intervene first by warning, second by repeating the warning, and third by having the bowler removed from the attack for the remainder of the innings. Bodyline constituted intimidatory bowling with the support of a ring of close leg-side fielders.

Jerk (or Jerking)

Archaic term relating to a doubtful means of delivery which may be caused by a sudden straightening of the arm and was subject to a call of 'no-ball' in older wordings of that law.

King pair

The worst of all possible calamities for a batsman: being dismissed first ball in each innings of a match.

Knock

A single innings played by a batsman.

Knock up

A batsman's net practice.

Lbw

Leg before wicket, one of the most controversial means of dismissal in cricket. Discussed in detail in Chapter 2.

Left handers

All terminology in this book relates to right handers. For left handers the game is a mirror image. The on side becomes the off side, in-swing the away swing, and off-break the leg-break and so on. Fielding teams usually cross sides for left-handed batsmen, and bowlers are required to chance direction if bowling to a similar field as for right handers. Bowlers are often treated to the variant term left armers, those who ply the trade of spinning the ball from the leg to off sides as orthodox, while those who spin the ball with a wrist action into the bat are described as unorthodox.

Leg break

A ball which moves from the leg side to the off side on pitching.

Leg cutter

A fast leg break produced by cutting the fingers down the side of the ball with the inswinger's grip. If combined with inswing it can be a devastating ball. Used by Dennis Lillee at the end of his career and with great effect by Merv Hughes.

Leg side

An alternative expression for on side.

Leg spinner

A ball which spins from the leg side to the off and is delivered with an action requiring a simultaneous flick of fingers and wrist.

Leg theory

Mode of bowling attack based on sharp swing to a close-set leg field it was originally an aggressive tactic but was perverted under Bodyline with its emphasis on intimidation. Modern forms of leg theory have been defensive measures to prevent batsmen from using their off side strokes.

Leg trap

Fielders placed in catching positions for inswing bowlers, fast bowlers pitching short, and off spinners in the hope that batsmen will be induced to give a catch to one of them.

Let fly

The action of a batsman playing a single free-flowing stroke after having been concentrating on defence.

Line and length
The major requisite of good bowling.
Lob
(1) A throw from the outfield which lands in the wicket-keeper's gloves.
(2) An antiquated form of underarm bowling which used to aim at dropping the ball on the top of the wicket from a high trajectory.
Lolly
A simple catch.
Long handle
To use the long handle means to apply maximum power in a stroke by fully extending and freely swinging the bat.
Long hop
A short pitched ball innocuous ball. A rank long hop is even worse.
Long stop
Fielding position directly behind the wicket-keeper. A necessity in the days of rough wickets, uneven grounds and before the advent of pads for the protection of wicket-keepers. The job of the long stop was to reduce the number of runs scored from byes.
Loop
A flighted trajectory used by a variety of slow bowlers.
Loose ball
A ball which lacks good line and length.
Lunch
An interval usually of forty minutes taken after the first two hours play. A few remarkable batsmen have made 100 runs before lunch.
Maiden
An over from which no runs are scored.
Mankad
Describes the action of a bowler effecting a run out by removing the bails at the non-strikers' end as part of his delivery action, and with the non-striker out of his crease through having backed up prematurely. Named after the Indian all-rounder Vinoo Mankad who ran out Australian opener Bill Brown by this means in the Second Test at Sydney in 1947-48.
MCC
(1) The Marylebone Cricket Club at Lord's is the main law making body of cricket.
(2) The Melbourne Cricket Club is often known as the other MCC.

Middle

(1) Another name for the pitch or wicket in the middle of the playing arena.

(2) Hit the ball in the middle of the bat.

Movement

Relates to any movement through the air by swing or off the pitch by cut, seam or spin.

New ball

Fielding sides begin first-class matches in Australia with a new ball and the captain of such teams may request another new ball after a designated number of overs. A team also has a new ball at the start of each new innings. Being shiny and hard it favours pace bowlers by swinging further, bouncing higher and seaming more off the wicket than an old ball. By contrast spin bowlers find it more difficult to grip although some like the extra bounce.

Nibble

A tentative stroke made at a ball which passes outside the off stump without contact being made.

Nick

See **Snick**.

Nightwatchman

Term for a late order batsman sent in late in the day well above his normal position. The hope is that he will survive and protect a better batsman until the following morning. Sometimes the nightwatchman thrives on responsibility as in the case of Jason Gillespie who made a Test double-century against Bangladesh at Chittagong in April 2006. Steve Waugh banned the nightwatchman during his highly successful reign as Test captain but it has been restored by his successor Ricky Ponting.

Nip

A bowler who gains greater pace from the wicket than his action would appear to indicate.

No-ball

A call of 'no-ball' is made for a variety of infringements and is a penalty ball. If not scored off it is recorded as an extra and debited against the bowler. A batsman may strike a no-ball for runs without being dismissed by any of the common methods except being run out.

Non-striker

The batsman not on strike.

Non-walker

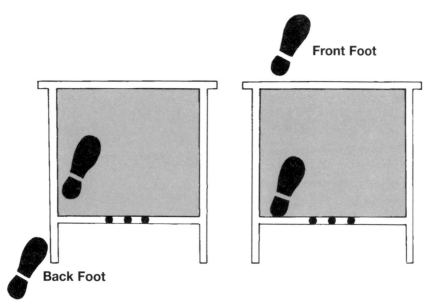

Front Foot

Back Foot

(1) Back foot outside the return crease   (2) Front foot over popping crease

No-ball

A batsman's who waits for the umpire's decision when an appeal is made for his decision. See **Walker**.

Occupying the crease

Describes a batsman who stays in a long time without making many runs.

Off cutter

A fast off break produced by cutting the fingers down one side of the ball as distinct from the finger spinner's method of tweaking the ball.

Off side

The half of a cricket field on the side away from the batsman.

Off the glove

A deflection which strikes one of the gloves and not the bat of the batsman, but if caught by the wicket-keeper or a fielder is out.

Off theory

Mode of attack based on bowling at the off stump or just outside it to a primarily off side field. Most fast bowlers in the world use off theory, packing the off side with slips and gully fielders.

Off the pad

A deflection which strikes and may bring leg byes but if caught is not out.

On his way

A term with opposite meanings.

(1) A batsman who has just been dismissed and is on his way back to the dressing room.

(2) A batsman who has broken his defensive shackles and is on his way to a century.

On side

The half of a cricket field on the side of the batsmen's legs.

On strike

A batsman receiving the bowler.

Openers

(1) The two batsmen who start the innings for the batting side.

(2) The opening bowlers are those who take the new ball opposing them.

Open one's account

Start scoring.

Open the shoulders

A variant of taking the long handle, simply swinging the bat freely in making an attacking stroke.

Out

(1) A batsman who has been dismissed.

(2) The dismissal of the entire team.

Outer

Open areas of grounds as distinct from grandstands.

Outfield

Fielding positions which are located nearer the boundary than the pitch, and are employed for primarily defensive reasons.

Out of his ground

A batsman who is outside his crease when a ball is in play but which raises most excitement in the event of a possible run out or stumping.

Over

A bowling unit of 6 balls delivered before the attack is switched to the other end. The number of balls has varied throughout cricket history: from 4 to 5 in 1889 and 6 in 1900. Australia used the 8 ball over virtually continuously between 1918 and 1979-80 and other Test-playing nations gave it a brief trial.

Over the wicket

Method of bowling with the delivery arm nearest the stumps.

Overthrows

Runs which benefit the batsman usually as a result of a fielder throwing the ball at the stumps in the hope of effecting a run out but with no fielder backing up.

Pace

(1) The measure of steps in a bowler's run up.

(2) The measure of speed of various bowlers.

Pad

Article of equipment worn on the legs for the protection of the batsman due to the strong emphasis on pace bowling in modern cricket. Thigh pads are also much more common than previously and chest padding is also worn.

Pad play

Unattractive form of defensive cricket where the batsman who is unsure of himself employs the pad instead of the bat in order to survive.

Pair

Being dismissed without scoring in each innings of a match. Short for pair of spectacles. Notable batsmen who began their Test careers in this way are Englishmen Dennis Amiss and Graham Gooch.

Pat

A soft defensive push of the bat.

Pickets

Many cricket grounds have wooden picket fences so a shot which hits the pickets has gone for four runs.

Pitch

The term has distinct meanings

(1) The strip on which a cricket match is played, alternatively called a Wicket.

(2) The spot where the ball hits the wicket when delivered leading to the expression full pitch and short pitch being applied.

(3) Although pitching in baseball involves throwing the ball it can also mean bowling legitimately.

Play in

A batsman who is described as playing himself in is generally playing defensively and straight while getting a feeling for the bowling and the pace of the pitch before attempting his attacking strokes.

Playing between the arc

Playing straight or in the arc between mid off and mid on.

Play on

PAT

PTT

A batsman who is bowled after first striking the ball and getting an edge onto his stumps.

Polishing the ball

Action practiced by pace bowlers in order to gain more movement through the air. Sometimes gives the appearance of merely being something to do and leads to an increase in dry cleaning bills.

Push

A stroke without power by which a batsman attempts to score runs by finding gaps in the field.

Push through

A tactical manoeuvre in which a bowler quickens his normal pace and if a spinner flights the ball less than usual.

Quicks (or **Quickies**)

A term for pace bowlers.

Quick single

A popular method of keeping the scoreboard moving as well as breaking up the field.

Rabbit

A batsman with little ability.

Rash stroke

One which puts the batsman at risk of losing his wicket.

Read (the spin or wicket)

To unravel supposed mysteries.

Return

A throw to either set of stumps from the field.

Roller (heavy or light)

Instruments used for evening the surface of the wicket.

Rough

Refers to the ground at each end of the pitch which may be cut up by bowlers' footmarks. A bowler pitching into such an area may extract abnormal lift or turn.

Roundarm

Ball delivered with an action where the bowling arm is shoulder height.

Round the wicket

To bowl with the delivery arm furthest from the stumps.

Runner

A batsman may use a substitute runner if he is ill or injured and first obtains the permission of the fielding captain to do so. When on strike

HEAVY ROLLER

the batsman can be stumped or run out at his end, but as a non-striker stands near the square leg umpire and takes no part in the game.

Running on the wicket

Batsmen run only on the edges of the pitch and bowlers may be warned by the umpires for running on the pitch. Failure to heed such warnings may result in a bowler being prohibited from bowling again during the team's innings.

Run of outs

A succession of small scores by a batsman.

Runs

The principal unit in the game and the means by which teams and individual scores are recorded and results of matches determined.

Sandshoe crusher

A type of **Yorker** likely to crush the batsmen's toes if he is wearing inappropriate footwear and is unable to ward off the ball with his bat.

Scratchy

Description of a batsman whose play lacks confidence.

Seamer

Predominantly a fast or medium pace bowler who moves the ball of the pitch by means of the ball striking the seam of the ball.

Seeing the ball like a football

Suggests a batsman in a confident frame of mind.

Send in

Action of a captain who, on winning the toss, invites his opponents to bat first.

Session

A period of play between the start of play and lunch, lunch and tea, and tea and the end of play. In Test matches these are each of two hours duration although often the last session is extended because of a mandatory provision to bowl 90 overs. In limited over matches each side bowls 50 overs in an extended period of three and half hours which may be designated morning, afternoon or evening depending on whether the game is played in the day or as a day-night game under lights.

Set

A batsman who is hitting the ball confidently. A batsman who is hitting the ball even more confidently is well set.

Shine

A new ball is shiny and swings through the air. Fast bowlers try to retain shine on the ball for as long as possible.

Shock ball

A surprise delivery.

Shock bowler

A bowler with wicket-taking abilities but whose effectiveness is greatest if bowled in short spells.

Shooter

A ball which shoots along the ground instead of bouncing. A nightmare for batsmen causing dismissals bowled and lbw.

Short run

(1) When running a batsman must ensure that he reaches his ground at the other end of the pitch before turning for another run. If he fails to do so a short run is signalled.

(2) Fast bowlers often cut their run significantly in order to conserve energy.

Shouldering arms

A batsman who raises his bat above his shoulders and allows the ball to pass without offering a stroke.

Shutters

Batsmen are said to be 'putting down the shutters' just before the end of play in order to bat again the following day. Some batsmen rarely lift them up.

Sight of the ball

The ability to follow its flight. To get a so-called early sight of the ball is one of the marks of a good batsman.

Slash

A wild stroke aimed through the off side and which often flies over the slips cordon.

Sledging

A form of gamesmanship involving swearing and belittling opponents with the aim of breaking concentration and bringing about dismissals.

Sling

A fast ball bowled with a roundarm action.

Slog

A wild stroke in any direction.

Smother

Defensive action employed by batsmen against spin bowlers involving getting over the top of the ball with a an angled bat.

Snick

A fine edge to the wicket-keeper or slips fielders. See also **Nick, Tickle**.

Snorter

A superb ball which defeats the batsman absolutely and sometimes is rewarded with his wicket. Occasionally referred to as a rip-snorter.

Soft hands

An aid to playing dead bat strokes.

Spell

A succession of overs delivered by a bowler or a rest from bowling.

Stance

How a batsman stands when facing the bowler. A two-eyed stance is used by some batsmen to improve their technique against the moving ball. While reducing the risk of being caught in slips it inhibits a batsman's ability to drive through the off side.

Stand

A run-scoring partnership between two batsmen.

Steal

Batsmen sometimes steal runs by fast thinking and a good understanding with their partner so that they get a head start on the fielders by making clever placements with their strokes.

Stock ball

The most common delivery in a particular bowler's repertoire.

Stock bowler

One who is required to deliver long spells (often in a defensive capacity) in order to allow the major shock bowlers to be suitably refreshed when introduced into the attack.

Stonewaller

A batsman who is defensive by inclination.

Straight bat

The correct method of playing drives and all defensive strokes.

Striker

The batsman receiving the bowling.

Stumps

(1) Two sets of three slim cylindrical wooden uprights which stand 71.1 cm (28 inches) high and are 22.86 cm (9 inches) wide. The stumps have grooves carved in the tops of them so that twh bails may be fitted. The stumps are located at each end of the pitch and at a distance of 20.12 metres (22 yards). See **Wicket**.

(2) An alternative expression for **Close of Play**.

Substitute

Replacement fielder or runner for player who is indisposed owing to illness or injury.

Swerve

A variety of swing and practised by slow bowlers as an aid to spin. The ability to swerve the ball one way in the air and spin it back the other is a mark of a class bowler. See **Drift**.

Tail (or Tail end)

Batsmen who go in at the bottom of the order.

Tearaway

A sometimes erratic fast bowler who can only sustain his pace for a few overs.

Teaser

A ball which seems simpler than it is and causes confusion in the mind of the batsman.

Tea

Mid-afternoon break usually taken at 3.40pm for an interval of twenty minutes when the close of play is scheduled for 6.00pm.

Team

Cricket teams usually consist of eleven active players and a twelfth man.

Test match

Traditionally the highest form of international cricket played against full members of the International Cricket Conference. The countries besides Australia and England who played the first Test at Melbourne in 1877 are South Africa (1888-1970 and since 1992), the West Indies (1928), New Zealand (1930), India (1932), Pakistan (1954), Sri Lanka (1982), Zimbabwe (1992) and Bangladesh (2000).

Throw

(1) A return from a fielder.

(2) An illegal delivery by a bowler. See **No-ball**.

Throwing the bat around

An aggressive batting display

Tickle

See **Snick**.

Tie

The most exciting result in a cricket match when an equal total of runs is scored by each side.

Time wasting

Although the minimum of 90 overs must be bowled each day in a Test match, and 96 overs in Pura Cup matches there are still occasions where wastage occurs. Fast bowlers dawdle back to their marks, slow bowlers, fielders and captains also contribute to delays.

Ton

One hundred runs, a source of satisfaction to all batsmen.

Top Cod

An expression chorused by the fielding side to support a bowler who has delivered a good ball. Often repeated for emphasis to the greater annoyance of the batsman.

Top spin

A ball delivered by leg spin bowlers which gathers pace from the pitch and goes straight through, claiming many wickets bowled or lbw.

Toss

(1) All matches begin with two captains tossing a coin to decide which team will bat first.

(2) Colloquial term for bowl as in 'toss the ball up' which usually refers to slow bowling.

Touch

A very fine **Edge, Nick** or **Snick** that results in a catch to the wicket-keeper.

Track

A slang term for the **Pitch** or **Wicket**. See also **Flat track, Half tracker**.

Turn

Another name for spin.

Turner

A pitch which is conducive to spin.

Tweak/tweaker

A term applied to a finger spinner who gives the ball more spin or puts more revolutions on the ball than usual.

Twelfth man

Reserve player who may act as a substitute when required but who often only undertakes the duty of drink waiter.

Two paced

A wicket where the pace varies.

Umbrella field

An attacking arrangement of fielders in catching positions behind and on both sides of the wicket.

Unorthodox

(1) Abnormal and sometimes inspired play. When batting, driving well pitched up balls off the back foot, hitting across the line and against the spin may carry risks but bring rewards.

(2) Left arm wrist spin bowlers are often described as unorthodox but right arm wrist spinners are not.

Walker

A batsman who volunteers his own dismissal rather than waiting for the umpire's decision.

Wicket

The most frequently used term in cricket and the one with the most meanings:

(1) The targets consisting of the **Stumps** and **Bails**.

(2) The pitch or playing surface between the stumps and the area 2.64 metres (8 feet 8 inches) wide between the bowling creases.

(3) A dismissal in the sense of a wicket being taken or lost.

(4) A position in the batting order denoted by the number of wickets fallen.

Wrist spin

Where the predominant amount of spin is imparted by flicking the wrist. Right-arm leg-spinners all gain turn by such means.

Wrong'un.

Another term for **Bosey** and **Googly**.

Yorker

A ball which lands about the popping crease and passes the bat before the batsman can bring it down. A valuable strike weapon for fast bowlers.

Zero

See **Blob** or **Duck**.

Zooter

One of a number of make-believe deliveries supposedly bowled by Shane Warne.

Statistics

First-class cricket

1. Teams

Highest match aggregate	2736 runs for 38 wickets, Maharashtra v Bombay at Poona.	1948-49
Lowest match aggregate	105 for 31 wickets, MCC v Australia at Lord's.	1878
Highest team innings	1107, Victoria v New South Wales at Melbourne.	1926-27
Lowest team innings	12, Oxford University v MCC & Ground at Oxford.	1877
	12, Northamptonshire v Gloucestershire at Gloucester.	1907

2. Batting (individual)

Highest innings	501, B.C. Lara, Warwickshire v Durham at Edgbaston.	1994
Most runs in a career	61 237 (average 50.65), J.B. Hobbs, 834 matches.	1905-34
Highest average in a career	95.14 (28 067 runs), D.G. Bradman, 234 matches.	1927-48
Most centuries in a career	197, J.B. Hobbs	1905-34

Longest innings	16 hours 55 minutes	1999-2000
	271,R. Nayyar, Himachal Pradesh v	
	Jammu & Kashmir, Chamba.	

Fastest genuine century	35 minutes, P.G.H. Fender,	1920
	Surrey v Northamptonshire at	
	Northampton.	
	34 balls, D.W. Hookes,	1982-83
	South Australia v Victoria	
	at Adelaide.	

Most sixes in an innings	16, A. Symonds,	1995
	Gloucestershire v Glamorgan at	
	Abergavenny.	

3. Batting (partnerships)

First wicket	561, Waheed Mirza and	1976-77
	Mansoor Akhtar, Karachi Whites	
	v Quelta at Karachi.	

Second wicket	576, R.S. Mahanama and	1997
	S.T. Jayasuriya, Sri Lanka v	
	India at R. Premadasa	
	Stadium, Colombo.	

Third wicket	624, D.P.M.D. Jayawardene and	2006
	K.C. Sangakkara, Sir Lanka v	
	South Africa at Colombo.	

Fourth wicket	577, V.S. Hazare and	1946-47
	Gul Mahomed, Baroda v	
	Holkar at Baroda.	

Fifth wicket	464, M.E. Waugh and	1990-91
	S.R. Waugh, New South Wales	
	v Western Australia at Perth.	

Sixth wicket	487, G.A. Headley and	1931-32
	C.C. Passailaigue, Jamaica v Lord	
	Tennyson's XI at Kingston.	

Seventh wicket	460, Bhupinder Singh and	1994-95
	P. Dharman, Punjab v	
	Delhi at Delhi.	

Eighth wicket	433, A. Sims and V.T. Trumper, An Australian XI v Canterbury at Christchurch.	1913-14
Ninth wicket	283, A. Warren and J. Chapman, Derbyshire v Warwickshire at Blackwell.	1910
Tenth wicket	307, A.F. Kippax and J.E.H. Hooker, New South Wales v Victoria at Melbourne.	1928-29

4. Bowling

Best match performance	19 wickets for 90 runs, J.C. Laker, England v Australia at Old Trafford.	1956
Best innings performance	10 wickets for 10 runs, H. Verity, Yorkshire v Nottinghamshire at Headingley.	1932
Most wickets in a career	4187, W. Rhodes, 1110 matches.	1898-1930
Most hat-tricks in a career	7, D.V.P. Wright	1932-57
Most expensive match analysis	11 wickets for 428 runs, C.S. Nayudu, Holkar v Bombay at Bombay.	1944-45
Most expensive innings analysis	4 wickets for 362 runs, A.A. Mailey, New South Wales v Victoria at Melbourne.	1926-27
Most balls bowled in a match	917, C.S. Nayudu, Holkar v Bombay at Bombay.	1944-45
Most balls bowled in an innings	588, S. Ramadhin, West Indies v England at Edgbaston.	1957

5. Wicket-keeping

Most dismissals in a match	13 (11c, 2 st), W.R. James, Matabeleland v Mashonaland Country at Bulawayo,	1995-96

Most dismissals in an innings	9 (7c, 2st), W.R. James, Matabeleland v Mashonaland Country at Bulawayo.	1995-96
	9 (8c 1st), Tajit Rasheed, Habib Bank v PACQ at Gujranawala.	1992-93
Most dismissals in a career	1649 (1473c, 173 st), R.W. Taylor, 639 matches.	1960-88

6. Fielding

Most catches in a match	10, W.R. Hammond Gloucestershire v Surrey at Cheltenham.	1928
Most catches in an innings	7, M.J. Stewart. Surrey v Northhamptonshire at Northhampton.	1957
Most catches in a career	1018, F.E. Woolley, 978 matches.	1906-38

Test matches

1. Teams

Highest match aggregate	1981 runs for 35 wickets, South Africa v England at Durban.	1938-39
Lowest match aggregate	234 for 29 wickets, Australia v South Africa at Melbourne.	1931-32
Highest team innings	952 for 6 wickets (declared), Sri Lanka v India at R. Premadasa Stadium, Colombo.	1997
Lowest team innings	26, New Zealand v England at Auckland.	1954-55

2. Batting (individual)

Highest innings	400 not out, B.C. Lara, West Indies v England at St. John's.	2004

Most runs in a career	11 505 (average 52.05), B.C. Lara, 128 matches.	1990-
Highest average in a career	99.94 (6996 runs), D.G. Bradman, 52 matches.	1928-48
Most centuries in a career	35, S.R. Tendulkar	1989-
Longest innings	16 hours 10 minutes 337, Hanif Mohammed, Pakistan v West Indies at Bridgetown.	1957-58
Fastest century	70 minutes, J.M. Gregory, Australia v South Africa at Johannesburg,.	1921-22
	56 balls, I.V.A. Richards, West Indies v England, St. John's.	1986

3. Batting (partnerships)

First wicket	413, V. Mankad and P. Roy, India v New Zealand at Madras.	1955-56
Second wicket	576, R.S. Mahanama and S.T. Jayasuriya, Sri Lanka v India at R. Premadasa Stadium, Colombo.	1997
Third wicket	624, D.P.M.D. Jayawardene and K.C. Sangakkara, Sir Lanka v South Africa at Colombo.	2006
Fourth wicket	411, P.B.H. May and K.C. Sangakkara, Sir Lanka v West Indies at Edgbaston.	1957
Fifth wicket	405, S.G. Barnes and D.G. Bradman, Australia v England at Sydney.	1946-47
Sixth wicket	346, J.H.W. Fingleton and D.G. Bradman, Australia v England at Melbourne.	1936-37

Seventh wicket	347, D.StE. Atkinson and C.C. Depeiza, West Indies v Australia at Bridgetown.	1955
Eighth wicket	313, Saqlain Mushtaq and Wasim Akram, Pakistan v Zimbabwe at Sheikhupura.	1996-97
Ninth wicket	195, P.L. Symcox and M.V. Boucher, South Africa v Pakistan at Johannesburg.	1997-98
Tenth wicket	151, B.F. Hastings and R.O. Collinge, New Zealand v Pakistan at Auckland.	1972-73
	151, Mushtaq Ahmed and Azhar Mahmood, Pakistan v South Africa at Rawalpindi.	1997-98

4. Bowling

Best match performance	19 wickets for 90 runs, J.C. Laker, England v Australia at Old Trafford.	1956
Best innings performance	10 wickets for 53 runs, J.C. Laker, England v Australia at Old Trafford.	1956
Most wickets in a career	685, S.K. Warne	1992-
Most wickets in a series	49 (four Tests), S.F. Barnes, England v South Africa.	1913-14
Most balls bowled in a match	774, S. Ramadhin, West Indies v England at Edgbaston.	1957
Most balls bowled in an innings	588, S. Ramadhin, West Indies v England at Edgbaston.	1957

5. Wicket-keeping

Most dismissals in a match	11 (all caught), R.C. Russell, England v South Africa at Johannesburg.	1995-96
Most dismissals in an innings (all caught)	7, Wasim Bari, Pakistan v New Zealand at Auckland.	1978-79
	7, R.W. Taylor, England v India at Bombay.	1979-80
	7, I.D.S. Smith, New Zealand v Sri Lanka at Hamilton.	1990-91
	7, R.D. Jacobs, West Indies v Australia at Melbourne.	2000-01
Most dismissals in a series	28, R.W. Marsh, Australia v England.	1982-83
Most dismissals in a career	395 (366c 29 st), I.A. Healy, 119 Tests.	1988-99

6. Fielding

Most catches in a match	7, G.S. Chappell, Australia v England at Perth.	1974-75
	7, Yajurvindra Singh, India v England at Bangalore.	1976-77
	7, H.P. Tillakaratne, Sri Lanka v New Zealand at Colombo (SSC).	1992-93
	7, S.P. Fleming, New Zealand v Zimbabwe at Harare.	1997-98
	7, M.L. Hayden, Australia v Sri Lanka at Galle.	2003-04
Most catches in an innings	5, V.Y. Richardson, Australia v South Africa at Durban,	1935-36
	5, Yajurvindra Singh, India v England at Bangalore.	1976-77
	5, M. Azharuddin, India v Pakistan at Karachi.	1989-90
	5, K. Srikanth, India	1991-92

	v Australia at Perth.	
	5, S.P. Fleming, New Zealand v Zimbabwe at Harare.	1997-98
Most catches in a series	15, J.M. Gregory, Australia v England.	1920-21
Most catches in a career	181, M.E. Waugh, 128 Tests.	1991-2002

Limited-over international matches

1. Teams

Highest match aggregate	872 runs for 13 wickets from 99.5 overs, South Africa v Australia at Johannesburg.	2005-06
Lowest match aggregate	73 for 11 wickets, Canada v Sri Lanka at Paarl.	2002-03
Highest team innings	438 for 9 wickets, South Africa v Australia at Johannesburg.	2005-06
Lowest team innings	35, Zimbabwe v Sri Lanka at Harare.	2004

2. Batting (individual)

Highest innings	194, Saeed Anwar, Pakistan v India at Chennai.	1996-97
Most runs in a career	14 146 (average 44.20), S.R. Tendulkar, 362 matches.	1989-
Highest average in a career	53.58 (6912 runs), M.G. Bevan, 242 matches.	1994-
Most centuries in a career	39, S.R. Tendulkar, 362 matches.	1989-
Fastest century	37 balls, Shahid Afridi (102), Pakistan v Sri Lanka at Nairobi.	1996-97
Most sixes in a career	215, Shahid Afridi, 225 matches,	1996-
Most sixes in an innings	11, S.T. Jayasuriya (134), Sri Lanka v Pakistan at Singapore.	1995-96
	11, Shahid Afridi (102), Pakistan v Sri Lanka at Nairobi.	1996-97

| Highest strike rate
(Runs per 100 balls) | 108.16 (4824 runs),
Shahid Afridi, 225 matches. | 1996- |

3. Batting (partnerships)

First wicket	286, W.U. Tharanga and S.T. Jayasuriya, Sri Lanka v England at Headingley.	2006
Second wicket	331, R. Dravid and S.R. Tendulkar, India v New Zealand at Hyderabad.	1999-2000
Third wicket	237*, R. Dravid and S.R. Tendulkar, India v Kenya at Bristol.	1999
Fourth wicket	275*, M. Azharuddin and A. Jadeja, India v Zimbabwe at Cuttack.	1997-98
Fifth wicket	223, A. Jadeja and M. Azharuddin, India v Sri Lanka at R. Premadasa, Stadium, Colombo.	1997
Sixth wicket	161 M. Odumbe and A.V. Vadher, Kenya v Sri Lanka at Southampton.	1999
Seventh wicket	130, H.H. Streak and A. Flower, Zimbabwe v England at Harare.	2001-02
Eighth wicket	119, S.K, Warne and P.R. Reiffel, Australia v South Africa at Port Elizabeth.	1993-94
Ninth wicket	126*, Kapil Dev and S.M.H. Kirmani, India v Zimbabwe at Tunbridge Wells.	1983
Tenth wicket	106*, I.V.A. Richards and M. Holding, West Indies v England at Old Trafford.	1984

4. Bowling

Best innings performance	8 wickets for 19 runs, W.P.U.J.C. Vaas, Sri Lanka v Zimbabwe at Colombo (SSC).	2001-02
Most wickets in a career	502 (average 23.52), Wasim Akram, 356 matches.	1984-2003
Most 5 wickets in an innings	13, Waqar Younis, 262 matches.	1989-2003
Best average in a career	18.84 (146 wickets), Joel Garner, 98 matches.	1977-87
Best economy rate in a career (runs per over)	3.09 (146 wickets), Joel Garner, 98 matches.	1977-87
Best economy rate in an innings	4 wickets for 3 runs (10 overs 8 maidens), P.V. Simmons, West Indies v Pakistan at Sydney.	1992-93
Most expensive analysis	0 wickets for 113 runs (10 overs), M.L. Lewis, Australia v South Africa at Johannesburg.	2005-06

5. Wicket-keeping

Most dismissals in an innings match	6 (6c), A.C. Gilchrist, Australia v South Africa at Cape Town.	1999-2000
	6 (6c), A.J. Stewart, England v Zimbabwe at Old Trafford.	2000
	6 (5c 1st), R.D. Jacobs, West Indies v Sri Lanka at Colombo (RPS).	2001-02
	6 (5c 1st), A.C. Gilchrist, Australia v England at Sydney.	2002-03
	6 (6c), A.C. Gilchrist, Australia v Namibia at Potchefstroom,	2003
	6 (6c), A.C. Gilchrist, Australia v Sri Lanka at Colombo (RPS).	2003-04

| Most dismissals in a career | 393 (348c 45st), A.C. Gilchrist, 242 matches. | 1996- |

6. Fielding

| Most catches in an innings | 5, J.N. Rhodes, South Africa v West Indies at Mumbai. | 1993-94 |
| Most catches in a career | 156, M Azharuddin, 334 matches. | 1985-2000 |